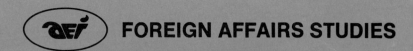 FOREIGN AFFAIRS STUDIES

WORLD FOOD PROBLEMS AND PROSPECTS

D. Gale Johnson

WORLD FOOD PROBLEMS
AND PROSPECTS

WORLD FOOD PROBLEMS
AND PROSPECTS

D. Gale Johnson

June 1975

American Enterprise Institute for Public Policy Research
Washington, D. C.

D. Gale Johnson is professor of economics at the University of Chicago.

ISBN 0-8447-3165-X

Foreign Affairs Study 20, June 1975

Library of Congress Catalog Card No. 75-13927

Printed in the United States of America

CONTENTS

1
INTRODUCTION AND SUMMARY

World food problems have become issues of broad concern. The World Food Conference in Rome in November 1974 was only the most prominent and spectacular indication of the interest expressed by many throughout the world. Malnutrition, starvation, and famine are now subjects of ordinary conversation. Few can fail to be distressed by pictures of children with swollen bellies and of gaunt adults who appear to be near death. One of our reactions to the pitiful circumstances in which many of the world's poor find themselves is a sense of helplessness. In a recent nationwide television program on hunger, a question that kept arising was what a single American family could do to help, and the unspoken answer was that very little could be done. The problems seemed so enormous that whatever one family could do would be of no significance.

Focus of the Study

In this study I have tried to address a number of actual or claimed world food problems. There is no single world food problem or single solution. Instead, there is a series of important questions which should be asked. Briefly, the questions are the following:

1) What were the major causes of the very large price increases of food products, especially the grains, in 1973 and 1974 and the shortfalls in food supplies in several low-income countries?
2) Is affluence—the high rates of food consumption in the industrial countries—a threat to the poor?
3) Is the world faced with substantially higher food prices over the next decade than during the decade prior to 1973?

1

4) Does the virtual disappearance of grain reserves mean that the world will be faced with substantially greater variability in food supplies and prices than during the two decades prior to 1973?
5) Are there adequate resources to increase the production of food so that it can at least keep pace with population growth in the developing countries?
6) Can a significant improvement in the per capita food supplies of the developing countries take place without a decline in population growth rates?
7) Does the political will exist in the United States, in the other industrial countries, or in the developing countries to undertake the measures required to increase world food output significantly?

Summary of Findings

The food shortages and the high prices of 1973 and 1974 are not the first difficulties of this sort that the world has witnessed. It is often forgotten that during three different periods within the last eight decades sober and competent individuals have raised the specter of famine—not in the developing countries, but in England and the United States. In the mid-1960s, for example, a series of poor crops in Asia and the Soviet Union led many to believe that a large fraction of the world's population faced food deprivation and starvation. Within two years, however, grain stocks had increased to levels considered burdensome by the major grain exporters, and real grain prices received by farmers in the United States fell to the lowest levels since 1929, except for 1931 and 1932.

The food crisis of 1973 and 1974 was the result of many factors occurring in a relatively brief span of time. For the first time in twenty years world grain production had declined because of relatively poor crops in Asia and the Soviet Union. Production recovered toward the end of 1973 but declined again in 1974. However, the shortfalls were relatively small and, in the absence of other factors, could not have accounted for the sharp price increases that occurred. Other factors included the simultaneous economic boom in the industrial economies and the continued increase in cattle herds throughout the world. The build-up of herds slowed the movement of cattle to market which, in turn, increased meat and livestock prices and the demand for grain. But the major factor in the doubling and trebling of grain prices was governmental policies in many countries that prevented the price system from rationing the available supplies. In countries with a large fraction of the world's population, grain prices were not permitted to increase to reflect the shortfalls in production and the depletion of grain reserves. Thus, the price-increasing factors were concentrated in the international grain markets, which had to absorb most of the production shortfalls and the expanding world demand. In spite of higher grain prices in international markets, the consumption of grain in most industrial countries was greater in 1973 and 1974 than in the years when international grain prices were substantially lower. In other words, there was very little sharing of the small reduction in grain production.

Affluence—or increasing per capita income—in the industrial countries has been blamed for the shortfalls in food availability in the developing countries. Consumers in the high-income countries have been told that they should reduce their consumption in order to make more food available to the poorer countries. But if there is a relation between increasing per capita incomes in the industrial countries and the availability of food to the developing countries, it has been instead to increase the food supplies of the latter. Affluence affects both the demand for and the supply of food, and for the past half-century the effect on supply has been greater than the effect on demand. Grain supplies have increased and real grain prices have fallen over the past six decades as a result of research, the substitution of mechanical for animal power, and the falling real prices of fertilizer—all consequences of affluence. Had it not been the high level of demand for grain in the industrial countries, grain output would have been much smaller than it was or now is. Exports of grain from North America and Australia would thus have been much smaller than has been the case, and the large reserves that prevented major hardships in the mid-1960s and greatly alleviated them in 1973 and 1974 would not have been accumulated.

There is a real concern that the world has entered a period of permanently increased food prices. Higher prices for energy, the return of diverted cropland to production in the United States, high rates of population growth in the developing countries, and rising per capita incomes throughout the world are given as reasons for the reversal in the long-term decline in real farm prices. But in this study I conclude that high farm prices are not here to stay, except insofar as farm prices reflect the effects of inflation. Energy costs do not constitute a large fraction of the costs of producing food, and the return of diverted land had only a small effect on total grain production in the United States in the early 1970s. I expect that the long-term decline in real grain prices will reassert itself. One factor delaying this decline is the devaluation of the American dollar. The overvaluation of the dollar during the 1960s and early 1970s probably depressed grain prices in international markets by 10 to 15 percent. In terms of the combined interests of taxpayers and consumers in the United States, the effect of the devaluation of the dollar is likely to be small since government payments to farmers largely compensated for the effects of the overvaluation.

During the 1950s and 1960s, grain reserves that were accumulated in North America as a result of farm price policies provided a remarkable degree of price stability for the grains. The reserves were not a part of a conscious policy but were primarily the unwanted consequences of setting price supports above market equilibrium levels. A more satisfactory way of controlling price variations for grains, however, would be the establishment of free trade in grains. If this were done, there would be little need for reserves to stabilize supplies and prices. If there is little progress in removing barriers to trade in grain and other farm products and if grain reserves are not rebuilt to the levels that prevailed through the 1960s, there will be price instability in the future.

It is generally agreed that there is enormous potential for increasing food production in the developing countries. The cultivated area could be substantially increased, and yields per unit of land could be doubled within two decades if sufficient effort were made. Higher yields can be achieved by means that are already well understood—a much greater research effort in the developing countries, increased inputs such as fertilizer, insecticides, and herbicides, improvement and expansion of irrigation facilities, and the elimination of governmental policies that exploit the agricultural sector and rural people. We now have incontrovertible evidence that poor and illiterate farmers will respond, and quickly, to adequate incentives and will increase food production if given the opportunity. Farmers are as smart as the rest of us and as willing to change and to adopt new techniques of production. If there is conservatism and irrationality in the world, it is to be found much more often among governments than among farm people.

There are no reasons based on limitations of resources or on the technology and biology of food production that will prevent the population of the world from being more adequately fed a decade hence than in the years immediately before 1972. I believe that the world's population will be better fed a decade hence, although I am less confident about the realization of the potential for increased food

4

production than I am about the potential itself, even if current population growth rates continue.

A significant reduction in birth rates in the developing countries would make a major contribution to the improvement of per capita food supplies by the end of this century. If currently high birth rates and population growth rates do not decline, even major efforts to expand food production will have only a modest effect.

It remains to be seen if the political will exists to give food problems the continuing priority required to increase the growth rate of food production over that achieved in the past two decades.

World food problems are continuing ones, at least until per capita production and incomes in the developing countries increase substantially from current levels. Somehow it must be recognized that long-run efforts to solve such problems must be made. It should be accepted that programs or measures started now will need to continue until the end of this century. We must maintain our attention and efforts during periods of relative abundance, recognizing that, unless we do, such abundance will almost certainly be followed by relative scarcity and much human suffering. But I am quite fearful that when food supplies become more plentiful, as I am confident they will within a year or two (assuming average weather conditions), those who now give so much emphasis to the current critical situation will turn their attention elsewhere. If this happens, tragic consequences will be inevitable.

While I am cautiously optimistic that the world has the capacity to provide more and better food for an increasing population, the short-run food situation remains a serious one. Almost certainly, hunger, malnutrition, and starvation occurred in 1973 and 1974 as a consequence of reduced grain production and the manner in which the shortfalls were distributed among the world's population. A poor grain crop that occurs before grain reserves are rebuilt could result in much human misery.

2
WORLD FOOD PROBLEMS
IN PERSPECTIVE

It is not easy to achieve a perspective on the nature and extent of world food problems. Scare headlines and statements are common. There is considerable disagreement concerning the distress that exists in a number of developing countries. There are predictions that the world is entering an extended period of food scarcity and high prices.

The objective of this chapter is to provide some perspective on the world's food situation as of the mid-1970s. The first part of the chapter presents information concerning earlier anticipated and actual food difficulties. The second part presents evidence showing that there has been a slow but not unimportant improvement in per capita food supplies in the low-income countries of the world over the past two decades coupled with an extraordinary increase in life expectancy over the same period. It is also noted that one of mankind's most horrible scourges—famine—has been much less evident in this than in prior centuries.

Earlier Food Scares

The current world food scare is not the first, nor is it likely to be the last, for reasons that I will develop more fully later. Within the last eight decades there have been four periods when it appeared that part of the world was either in or about to enter a food crisis. It is noteworthy that the focus of the first three periods was not the developing countries but England and the United States.

Wheat Scarcity in England. Toward the end of the nineteenth century many well-informed individuals in England feared that the major component of their food supply, wheat, was seriously endangered by the continuing growth of demand in the face of an almost static supply.

Sir William Crookes used the occasion of his presidential address to the British Association for the Advancement of Science in 1898 to address the topic of food supply:

> My chief subject is of interest to the whole world—to every race—to every human being. It is of urgent importance to-day, it is a life and death question for generations to come. I mean the question of food supply. Many of my statements you may think are of the alarmist order; certainly they are depressing, but they are founded on stubborn facts. They show that England and all civilised nations stand in deadly peril of not having enough to eat. As mouths multiply, food resources dwindle.[1]

Later in his address he said:

> Practically there remains no uncultivated prairie land in the United States suitable for wheat-growing. The virgin land has been rapidly absorbed, until at present there is no land left for wheat without reducing the area for maize, hay, and other necessary crops. It is almost certain that within a generation the ever increasing population of the United States will consume all the wheat grown within its borders, and will be driven to import, and, like ourselves, will scramble for a lion's share of the wheat crop of the world.[2]

Joseph S. Davis, one of the world's outstanding agricultural economists and a long-time student of world wheat supply and demand, published a review of Crookes's projection in 1932. His analysis provides the background of Crookes's concern:

> Sir William Crookes (1832–1919) was no irresponsible sensationalist. He was one of the most eminent scientists of his generation, who had done notable work in both physics and chemistry. Because of what he was, what he said commanded high respect. His discussion rested on considerable study and correspondence. He pondered the criticisms it evoked. Though his address was replete with alarmist phrases, he disavowed any intent "to create a sensation, or to indulge in a 'cosmic scare.'" He sought "to treat the matter soberly and without exaggeration."
>
> In the background of the address lay a real wheat stringency, which stood out in sharp contrast to the preceding

[1] Sir William Crookes, *The Wheat Problem* (New York: G. P. Putnam's Sons, 1900), p. 6.

[2] Ibid., pp. 17–18.

abundance. In 1897, following reductions in wheat reserves, short crops of both wheat and rye were the rule in Europe and in most exporting countries as well. Wheat prices advanced materially, and the spectacular Leiter corner in the spring of 1898 drove them up sharply further, for a time. Widespread famine was reported in Russia and in parts of India. In Great Britain, the danger of food scarcity in the event of war had already evoked special concern, even in conservative grain and milling circles. Britain was importing some three-fourths of her wheat consumption requirements, and large quantities of other food stuffs as well. It is not surprising that Crookes could say, after a review of Britain's position: "The burning question of today is, What can the United Kingdom do to be reasonably safe from starvation in presence of two successive failures of the world's wheat harvest or against a hostile combination of European nations?"[3]

(As Professor Davis also pointed out, by the early 1930s the problem bothering both exporting and importing nations was not the earlier one of having too many mouths and too little wheat but rather that of the effects of a permanently lowered price of wheat.)[4] It may be noted that a royal commission was appointed in 1903 to study the problem of food supply in time of war and that much of the testimony dealt with the precariousness of Britain's food supply for the long term, war or no war.[5]

One final comment about Crookes. He was not completely pessimistic about the future wheat supply. His purpose appeared to be not to spread alarm but to induce his scientific colleagues and British politicians to seek solutions to the wheat problem, in particular by providing the necessary conditions for significantly increasing wheat yields. "I have said that starvation may be averted through the laboratory. Before we are in the grip of actual dearth the Chemist will step in and postpone the day of famine to so distant a period that we, and our sons and grandsons, may legitimately live without undue solicitude for the future."[6] He was predicting the economically feasible fixation of atmospheric nitrogen. At that time, he was already confident that nitrogen fixation was possible, but he

---

[3] Joseph S. Davis, *On Agricultural Policy, 1926-1938* (Stanford, Calif.: Stanford University, Food Research Institute, 1939), pp. 4-5.

[4] Ibid., p. 4.

[5] Great Britain, *Royal Commission on Supply of Food and Raw Materials in Time of War*, 3 vols. (London: His Majesty's Stationery Office, 1905).

[6] Crookes, *The Wheat Problem*, p. 34.

was uncertain whether it could be done at a low enough cost to make the product economical as a fertilizer. At least one source credits Sir William as the inventor of the process for the fixation of atmospheric nitrogen. Not only did Sir William talk about a possible solution, but unlike most of us he made a major contribution to that solution—although in the early years of the century the application of nitrogen fertilizers to wheat contributed very little to increased output. Other factors, such as a greater expansion of wheat acreage than he projected, the substitution of mechanical for animal power, and the substitution of livestock products for wheat in human diets, were primarily responsible for changing a world wheat shortage into a disturbing excess of supply for numerous efforts by governments to protect their wheat producers.

The United States in the Early 1920s. The *Agricultural Yearbook, 1923*, a publication of the U.S. Department of Agriculture, carried a lengthy article entitled "The Utilization of Our Lands for Crops, Pasture, and Forests." While the conclusions were stated in guarded terms, the authors were clearly concerned about the capacity of the United States to feed a population of 150 million. Some indication of their concern is supplied by the following.

> . . . the growth of our population has resulted in an ever-increasing scarcity of our available land area, and it is important to consider some of the evidence of this scarcity. . . .
> The growing scarcity of land available for grazing livestock is reflected in the statistics of livestock. The per capita number of livestock in 1922 was less than two-thirds that in 1894. . . .
> The trend in the value of farm land up to 1920 appears to confirm the conclusion, supported also by other facts, that the nation reached and passed the apogee of agricultural land supply in proportion to population about three decades ago, and that we have entered a period which will necessarily be marked by a continually increasing scarcity of land.[7]

The authors then argued that the United States was faced with the alternatives of significantly increasing yields per unit of land or reducing per capita consumption. Higher yields were possible but only through much greater expenditures per unit of output, including

---

[7] L. C. Gray et al., "The Utilization of Our Lands for Crops, Pasture, and Forests," *Agriculture Yearbook, 1923* (Washington, D.C.: U.S. Government Printing Office, 1924), pp. 433, 438, 442.

10

expenditures on labor.[8] Unless "exceptional progress in scientific invention and discovery" occurred, we might "need to increase considerably the proportion of our population engaged in agriculture."[9] And such progress was not likely to come about for the next several decades. Nevertheless, the part of the nation's labor force engaged in agriculture declined from 27 percent in 1927 to approximately 4 percent today.[10]

The authors were highly skeptical that productivity could be increased enough to permit existing land resources to meet the requirements of 150 million people for food and forest products:

> To increase our average crop production per acre 47 percent may sound easy, but when we remember that this is an average increase to be attained for all of the crop land of the United States, the magnitude of the task that must be accomplished [to provide food for a population of 150 million] in perhaps little more than three decades . . . appears stupendous. Moreover, it should be noted that our record thus far indicates a very slow rate of progress in . . . increased yield per acre, whereas, on the other hand, the increasing scarcity of grazing land has already resulted in a considerable decrease in number of livestock per capita.[11]

Thus, their conclusion was that the nation, although it might achieve some increase in productivity, would find it necessary to reduce per capita consumption of food.[12]

The U.S. population reached 150 million in 1950, but crop yields on harvested land had not increased by 47 percent (although they did so by 1960).[13] On the other hand, per capita consumption had not declined by 1950 either.[14] One important source of error in

---

[8] Ibid., pp. 475-79.

[9] Ibid., p. 478.

[10] U.S. Bureau of the Census, *Historical Statistics of the United States: Colonial Times to 1957* (Washington, D.C.: U.S. Government Printing Office, 1960), p. 73; and U.S. Bureau of the Census, *Statistical Abstract of the United States, 1972* (Washington, D.C.: U.S. Government Printing Office, 1973), p. 216.

[11] Gray et al., "The Utilization of Our Lands," p. 489.

[12] Ibid., pp. 492-96.

[13] U.S. Department of Agriculture, *Changes in Farm Production and Efficiency: A Summary Report, 1964*, Statistical Bulletin, no. 233, revised July 1964, pp. 15-16.

[14] Economic Research Service, U.S. Department of Agriculture, *U.S. Food Consumption: Sources of Data and Trends, 1909-63*, Statistical Bulletin, no. 364, 1965, pp. 18-19, 25-26. The per capita consumption of meat, poultry, and fish increased from 160.3 pounds in 1920 to 176.7 pounds in 1950. The per capita consumption of eggs increased from 36.3 pounds to 48.5 pounds, and the consumption of dairy products (in terms of fluid milk equivalent) remained approximately unchanged—736 pounds in 1920 and 740 pounds in 1950.

the projection by Gray and his colleagues was the failure to foresee the replacement of animal power by tractors, which was essentially completed by 1950.

The Fifth Plate. The rapid increase in U.S. population during the last half of the 1940s was quite unexpected and by 1950 had resulted in a substantial upward revision of population estimates for 1960 and 1970. A rather minor food scare was generated, and the theme of it was the "fifth plate." The fifth plate was the 20 percent increase in population that was expected by 1960.

The Food Crisis in the 1960s. The early and mid-1960s saw a combination of events that placed a significant strain on the world food supply. Following a poor grain crop in 1960, China entered the world grain markets as a major importer of wheat. The Soviet Union, which was a net grain exporter of about 5 million tons annually from 1960 to 1962, became a net grain importer of the same magnitude over the next three years, following poor grain crops in 1963 and 1965. India had small grain crops in both 1965 and 1966,[15] and massive shipments of grain were required to prevent starvation there.

The total stocks of grain of the five major exporters (United States, Canada, Argentina, Australia, and the European Community) declined from 150 million tons in 1961 to 80 million tons in 1967.[16] Thus, it is perhaps not surprising that the probability of continuing food stringency, especially in the developing countries, was feared to be very great.

One who viewed the situation with alarm was Lester R. Brown. After commenting on declines in per capita food production in the developing countries after 1960, he noted the increasing dependence of the developing regions upon grain imports. He then concluded:

> The less developed world is losing the capacity to feed itself. Stated otherwise, the less-developed world is no longer able to provide enough food for large numbers of people being added each year. A growing part of each year's population increase is being sustained by food shipments coming from the developed world, principally North America, and largely under concessional terms.
>
> Why is the less developed world losing the capacity to feed itself? The cause of this disturbing trend can be de-

---

[15] Economic Research Service, U.S. Department of Agriculture, *World Agricultural Situation*, WAS-1, November 1970, pp. 9, 11.

[16] Ibid., p. 10.

scribed in simple terms. Historically, traditional societies increased food output along with population by simply expanding the area under cultivation. But now many densely populated, less-developed countries with rapidly growing populations have relatively little new land that can be readily brought under cultivation. Thus, additional food output must come largely from raising yields per acre. Herein lies the problem, for less-developed countries are not, almost by definition, well prepared to do this.[17]

Fortunately, the food crisis of the mid-1960s was of short duration. Grain crops in India and Pakistan were excellent in both 1967 and 1968, and world grain production in 1967 exceeded the 1965 level by 105 million tons, or by 12 percent.[18] Grain stocks of the five major exporters increased from 80 million tons in 1967 to 118 million tons two years later.[19] Grain production, especially wheat production, expanded rapidly in the three largest exporting countries—Australia, Canada, and the United States—from 1967 through 1970. Grain prices declined. Farmers and governments reacted as one might expect. In the three largest exporters the land devoted to wheat production declined from 45.1 million hectares in 1968 to 38.8 million hectares in 1969 and to 29.4 million in 1970. Wheat production in these countries was 75.4 million tons in 1968 and 54.2 million tons in 1970.[20]

In late 1968, in the midst of this rapidly changing situation, Lester Brown made a remarkable statement:

> . . . the world has recently entered a new agricultural era. It is difficult to date precisely this new era since many of the contributing factors have been years in the making. But in terms of measurable phenomena such as the sudden sweeping advances in food production in several major developing countries, the old era ended in 1966 and the new began in 1967.[21]

---

[17] Lester R. Brown, "World Population Growth, Food Needs, and Production Problems," paper presented at the annual convention of the American Society of Agronomy in Kansas City, Mo., November 17, 1964, p. 5.

[18] Economic Research Service, *World Agricultural Situation*, WAS-2, November 1971, p. 8. Rice was included as paddy or rough rice.

[19] Ibid., p. 10.

[20] U.S. Department of Agriculture, *Agricultural Statistics, 1970*, pp. 5-6, and *Agricultural Statistics, 1972*, pp. 5-6.

[21] Lester R. Brown, "A New Era in World Agriculture" (USDA 3773-68), paper presented at the symposium on World Population and Food Supply, Kansas State University, Manhattan, Kans., December 3, 1968, p. 1.

Later in the same paper he said:

> Are the recent agricultural advances a temporary phenomenon, or a new trend? They appear to be the latter. The agricultural revolution seems to have gone too far now to be arrested. Too much is at stake, too much has been invested, the expectations of too many people have been aroused. The agricultural revolution in Asia should not, therefore, be viewed as an event but as the beginning of a process—the eventual modernization of Asia.[22]

It is now clear that Brown swung too far in both directions. He was too pessimistic in 1964 and too optimistic in 1968. The so-called Green Revolution did not solve all the agricultural problems of the developing countries. The development of new high-yielding varieties proved that it was possible to achieve significant yield increases. Subsequent events have shown that little can be taken for granted in agriculture and food. Continuing and sustained effort is required if there is to be steady growth in food production, and there was no continuing and sustained effort from 1968 through 1974.

Recent Trends in Food Production

There are two main sources of data on world food production—the Food and Agriculture Organization of the United Nations (FAO) and the U.S. Department of Agriculture (USDA). Both sources agree that during the past two decades per capita food production has increased in the developing or low-income countries. In view of this, the persistence of the idea that the food situation in low-income countries is deteriorating is surprising.

It is true that the improvement in per capita food production has been modest. The FAO data, presented in Table 1, indicate that for the period from 1952 through 1972 per capita food production in the developing market economies increased at an annual rate of approximately 0.4 percent. The USDA data, presented in Table 2, convey approximately the same rate of improvement.

The Preparatory Committee of the World Food Conference held in Rome in 1974 gave its assessment of the growth of food production during the two-decade period as follows:

> The fact that for so long a period food production in the developing countries as a whole has kept ahead of a rate of

---

[22] Ibid., p. 14.

Table 1

GROWTH RATE OF FOOD PRODUCTION IN RELATION TO POPULATION IN WORLD AND MAIN REGIONS (FAO DATA), 1952–62 AND 1962–72

(percent per year) a

Type of Economy	1952–62			1962–72		
	Population	Food production		Population	Food production	
		Total	Per capita		Total	Per capita
Developed market economies b	1.2	2.5	1.3	1.0	2.4	1.4
Western Europe	.8	2.9	2.1	.8	2.2	1.4
North America	1.8	1.9	.1	1.2	2.4	1.2
Oceania	2.2	3.1	.9	2.0	2.7	.7
Eastern Europe and USSR	1.5	4.5	3.0	1.0	3.5	2.5
Total developed countries	1.3	3.1	1.8	1.0	2.7	1.7
Developing market economies b	2.4	3.1	.7	2.5	2.7	.2
Africa	2.2	2.2	—	2.5	2.7	.2
Far East	2.3	3.1	.8	2.5	2.7	.2
Latin America	2.8	3.2	.4	2.9	3.1	.2
Near East	2.6	3.4	.8	2.8	3.0	.2
Asian centrally planned economies	1.8	3.2	1.4	1.9	2.6	.7
Total developing countries	2.4	3.1	.7	2.4	2.7	.3
World	2.0	3.1	1.1	1.9	2.7	.8

a Trend rate of growth of food production, compound interest.
b Including countries in other regions not specified.
Source: World Food Conference, United Nations, *Assessment of the World Food Situation, Present and Future*, E/CONF. 65/3, 1974, Table 4.

Table 2
INDICES OF WORLD POPULATION AND FOOD PRODUCTION (USDA DATA), 1954–73 [a]
(index numbers, 1961–65 average = 100)

Calendar Year	World			Developed Countries			Developing Countries		
	Popu-lation	Food production		Popu-lation	Food production		Popu-lation	Food production	
		Total	Per capita		Total	Per capita		Total	Per capita
1954	84.2	77	91	89.1	77	86	80.6	77	96
1955	85.7	80	93	90.3	81	90	82.5	78	95
1956	87.3	84	96	91.5	85	93	84.4	82	97
1957	89.0	85	96	92.7	86	93	86.3	83	96
1958	90.7	90	99	93.9	91	97	88.4	87	98
1959	92.4	91	98	95.1	92	97	90.5	89	98
1960	94.2	94	100	96.3	96	100	92.8	92	99
1961	96.1	95	99	97.5	95	97	95.1	94	99
1962	98.0	98	100	98.9	98	99	97.5	97	100
1963	100.0	100	100	100.1	99	99	99.9	100	100
1964	101.9	103	101	101.2	103	102	102.4	104	102
1965	103.9	104	100	102.3	104	102	105.0	104	99
1966	105.9	109	103	103.4	111	107	107.7	106	98
1967	107.9	114	106	104.3	115	110	110.4	111	101
1968	109.9	118	107	105.3	119	113	113.2	115	102
1969	112.0	118	105	106.3	117	110	116.1	121	104
1970	114.2	121	106	107.3	119	111	119.0	126	106
1971	116.4	126	108	108.3	125	115	122.1	128	105
1972	118.7	124	104	109.3	124	113	125.3	125	100
1973	120.9	133	110	110.2	133	121	128.5	132	103

[a] World excluding Communist Asia; revised March 1974.

Source: Economic Research Service, U.S. Department of Agriculture, *The World Food Situation and Prospects to 1985*, Foreign Agricultural Economic Report, no. 98, December 1974, p. 2.

16

population growth that is unprecedented in world history is a tremendous achievement. Furthermore, food production in these countries in 1972 was 20 percent greater than in 1966, the previous year of widespread bad weather, so that even between the troughs of the longer-term trend production has outpaced population growth.[23]

The Diminishing Incidence of Famine

Famine is the most horrible of the manifestations of food insufficiency. Deaths during famines are not due solely to starvation. Historically, famines have been associated with epidemics of smallpox, cholera, typhus, or the plague. While famines are usually associated with crop failures, war and civil disturbances have often been directly or indirectly responsible.

We might be inclined to deduce from the pictorial evidence of famine that we have seen recently on television, in newspapers, and in magazines that the world is more prone to famine now than it used to be. But the evidence is clearly to the contrary. Both the percentage of the world's population afflicted by famine in recent decades and the absolute numbers have been relatively small compared with those occurring in those earlier periods of history for which we have reasonably reliable estimates of famine deaths.

There has been a rather substantial reduction in the incidence of famine during the past century. During the last quarter of the nineteenth century perhaps 20 million to 25 million died from famine.[24] If an adjustment for population increase is made, a comparable figure for the third quarter of this century would be at least 50 million and for the quarter century we are now entering at least 75 million. For the entire twentieth century to the present, there have probably been between 12 million and 15 million famine deaths, and many, if not the majority, were due to deliberate governmental policy, official mismanagement, or war and not to serious crop failure.

The decline in the incidence of famine has resulted only in part from improvements in per capita food production. Probably more important have been improvements in communication and transportation. Many of the famines that did occur could have been

[23] World Food Conference, United Nations, *Assessment of the World Food Situation, Present and Future*, E/CONF. 65/3, 1974, p. 31. The document was prepared under the general direction of S. Marei, Secretary-General of the World Food Conference, and presented as Item 8 of the Agenda of the World Food Conference.

[24] D. Gale Johnson, "Famine," *Encyclopaedia Britannica* (1970 ed.), pp. 58–59.

Table 3

LIFE EXPECTANCY AT BIRTH
(years)

Area	Circa 1950	1970–75	Percentage Change (approximate)
Developing countries	35–40	52	+40
Developed countries	62–65	71	+12
World	38–43	55	+35

Source: Bernard Berelson, *World Population: Status Report 1974*, Reports on Population/Family Planning of the Population Council, no. 15, January 1974, p. 7.

prevented or largely alleviated if the world had known of their existence in time or if there had been reasonably adequate means of transportation to the locale.

Increase in Life Expectancy

Those who believe that the food situation of the poorer people of the world has deteriorated during the past quarter-century have no satisfactory explanation for a development unprecedented in recorded history, namely, the dramatic increase in life expectancy in the developing countries. During the 1950s there were a number of developing countries in which life expectancy increased at a rate of approximately one year per year—a rate of increase never achieved in Western Europe or North America.[25] These developing countries were Chile, Mexico, and Ceylon. Others that approached this rate of increase were Taiwan (0.92), India (0.94), and Jamaica (0.84).

Table 3 provides summary data on changes in life expectancy for developing countries, developed countries, and the world for the period from roughly 1950 to 1970–75. The differential between life expectancy in the developed and developing countries declined from 70 percent in 1950 to 35 percent currently. The developing countries, as a group, have now achieved a level of life expectancy that is approximately the same as that achieved by the United States in 1910, England in 1905, France in 1915, Italy in 1925, and Japan in 1947.[26]

[25] D. Gale Johnson, *The Struggle against World Hunger*, Headline Series, no. 184 (New York: Foreign Policy Association, 1967), p. 13.

[26] Donald Bogue, *Principles of Demography* (New York: John Wiley and Sons, Inc., 1969), Table 16-7.

No one would claim that increased per capita food supplies were primarily responsible for these large increases in life expectancy. Other factors such as DDT (for the control of malaria) and improvements in sanitation and the safety of water supplies were undoubtedly far more important. But the increase in life expectancy almost certainly could not have occurred if there had been instead a deterioration in the quantity and quality of food.

The largest percentage declines in death rates occurred among the young.[27] Infants and children normally suffer first and most from a reduction of food availability. Those of us who decry the high rates of population growth in the developing countries should not forget that the increases in these rates have been due entirely to reductions in death rates and not at all to an increase in birth rates.[28] There has been an enormous reduction in human suffering that has gone largely unrecognized—the pain and grief of hundreds of millions of parents that have been avoided by the reduction in infant and child mortality. Thus, although the rapid growth of population has imposed costs, the benefits that have accrued from the factors causing this growth should not be ignored.

Nutrition

The *Assessment of the World Food Situation, Present and Future* by the 1974 World Food Conference provides a sober evaluation of the nutrition situation in the developing countries as of 1970. There are some encouraging factors, such as the declines in mortality referred to above.

The overall summary of the changes in consumption of food energy in the developing market economies showed that per capita energy consumption increased from 93 percent of estimated requirements in 1961 to 97 percent of calorie requirements in the period 1969–71.[29] Averages were used for the estimates for each time period and the changes between the two periods. Obviously, if the estimates are accurate, significant percentages of the population in the develop-

---

[27] Ibid., pp. 559-60, 584-90. Some examples of infant mortality rates (deaths before one year of age per thousand live births) in 1946-48 and 1963, respectively, are the following: Mexico, 103 and 68; Chile, 154 and 111; Costa Rica, 93 and 78; Malaya, 95 and 57; Singapore, 86 and 28; and Jamaica, 89 and 52.

[28] Bernard Berelson, with the collaboration of staff members of the Population Council, *World Population: Status Report 1974*, Reports on Population/Family Planning of the Population Council, no. 15, January 1974, pp. 6-9.

[29] World Food Conference, *Assessment of the World Food Situation*, p. 58.

ing market economies are consuming less than 90 percent of energy requirements.

Although one can be somewhat skeptical of the accuracy of the estimates of available food supplies and of calorie or energy requirements for the developing countries, there is little doubt that millions of individuals in the world have inadequate diets either more or less continuously throughout the year or during the season prior to the harvest of the major food crop. In the World Food Conference's assessment, it is estimated that approximately 25 percent of the population in the developing market economies have less than adequate protein and energy consumption.[30]

Less than a decade ago it was generally believed that there was a serious protein deficiency in the developing countries. It is now agreed that

> it seems unlikely that a dietary intake that is sufficient to cover the energy requirements will be insufficient to meet the requirements for protein. This means that protein deficiency in the absence of energy deficiency is not probable to occur, a possible exception being in populations that subsist on cassava, plantains, yams or breadfruit, foods that are extremely low in protein content.[31]

In other words, in most developing countries, consuming more food will correct both calorie and protein deficiencies. This conclusion may not apply to many infants and young children.

The implications of this new evidence are encouraging: that much of the malnutrion that exists may be overcome primarily by supplying more food of the same types now consumed, except for those populations whose diets consist largely of noncereal sources of calories. It is generally much easier and less costly to expand production of cereals, such as wheat, corn, and sorghum, than of high protein crops, such as beans and peas.

It seems clear that during the 1950s and 1960s there was a significant improvement in the nutritional status of the populations of the developing countries. The evidence is of several sorts—increased life expectancy, decreased infant mortality, and increased per capita food intake. But there is considerable room for more improvement, especially among the lower income groups—the lower two-fifths of the income distribution—within the developing countries.

---

[30] Ibid., p. 66.
[31] Ibid., p. 56.

20

3
THE FOOD CRISIS
OF 1973 AND 1974

If, as has been argued in the previous chapter, the food situation in the developing countries has been gradually improving over the past two decades, why did food difficulties and stringencies occur in 1973 and 1974? Why did international prices of grains and many other food products double, treble, and even quadruple?

Many explanations have been given and, indeed, several factors were responsible. If similar difficulties are to be prevented in the future, an accurate appraisal of the major causes is important. The most commonly cited causes of the food crisis are the decline in food and grain production in the period 1972–73, which was attributed to adverse weather over large areas of the world; the drastic reduction in the Peruvian anchovy catch in 1972, with little recovery since that date; the large purchases of grain by the Soviet Union in 1972; rising affluence during the 1960s, which significantly increased the demand for livestock products and thus for feed grains and oilseeds; the decline in world grain stocks as a percentage of consumption after 1968 as a result of deliberate actions taken in the United States, Canada, and Australia; and the various devaluations of the U.S. dollar, which contributed to an increase in commercial export demand.[1]

---

[1] Some of the many attempts to determine the causes of the food difficulties of 1973 and 1974 may be found in Dale E. Hathaway, "Food Prices and Inflation," *Brookings Papers on Economic Activity*, 1974, no. 1, pp. 83-102; U.S. Congress, Senate, Committee on Agriculture and Forestry, Subcommittee on Agricultural Production, Marketing, and Stabilization of Prices and on Foreign Agricultural Policy, *Hearings on U.S. and World Food Situation*, 93rd Cong., 1st sess., October 1973, especially the testimony by Don Paarlberg, Lester Brown, Norman Borlaug, and William C. Paddock; and World Food Conference, United Nations, *Assessment of the World Food Situation, Present and Future*, E/CONF. 65/3, 1974, pp. 15-23.

As I shall try to show, the causes listed above were not sufficient to have resulted in the very large increases in the prices of grain and other farm and food products that actually occurred between mid-1972 and 1974. This is not to say that these causes were unimportant or insignificant but simply that additional forces were at work.

Food and Grain Production in Recent Years

Tables 4 and 5 give estimates of food production, for the world and various regions, for 1969 through 1973. The FAO estimates indicate that world food production was the same in 1971 and 1972 (Table 4), while the USDA estimates indicate a decline of less than 2 percent (Table 5). On a per capita basis, the FAO data indicate a decrease of about 2 percent for 1972, while the USDA data show a 4 percent decline. For the developing market economies, FAO estimates that per capita food production declined by 3 percent between 1971 and 1972; for approximately the same group of countries, the USDA estimates a 4 percent reduction. Both series indicate a decline in per capita food production for the developed and developing countries, although the reduction is somewhat larger for the developing countries.

The two sets of estimates agree that per capita food production in 1973 was at least as great for the world as it was in 1971 and only slightly lower for the developing countries.

The USDA has estimated that direct consumption of grains provides approximately 52 percent of the total calories consumed by the world's population and 62 percent of those consumed in the developing countries.[2] Furthermore, international trade in grains is the major route by which food is transferred from one world region to another; two other but much less important sources of transfer are trade in vegetable oils and sugar. Since data for grain production and use are more accurate and complete than for other food products, they can provide insight into the current food situation.

Table 6 presents USDA estimates of world grain production and consumption, trends in production and consumption, and deviations of actual production and consumption from their trends. It is more useful to compare a given year's production or consumption with a trend value for that year than with production or consumption in the prior year, since production and consumption of grain for the

---

[2] Economic Research Service, U.S. Department of Agriculture, *The World Food Situation and Prospects to 1985*, Foreign Agricultural Economic Report, no. 98, December 1974, p. 49.

22

Table 4

INDICES OF TOTAL AND PER CAPITA FOOD PRODUCTION IN WORLD AND MAJOR REGIONS (FAO DATA), 1969–73

(index numbers, 1961–65 average = 100)

Type of Economy	Total Food Production					Per Capita Food Production				
	1969	1970	1971	1972	1973	1969	1970	1971	1972	1973
Developed market economies [a]	116	116	123	122	126	109	108	114	112	114
Western Europe	115	117	122	122	125	110	111	115	113	116
North America	115	113	124	122	125	107	104	113	110	112
Oceania	123	121	127	127	139	108	107	109	108	116
Eastern Europe and USSR	123	130	132	133	148	116	121	123	122	134
Total developed countries	118	121	127	126	134	111	112	117	116	121
Developing market economies [a]	119	124	125	125	130	102	103	102	99	100
Africa	118	121	124	126	122	102	102	102	100	95
Far East	118	124	124	120	130	102	104	102	96	101
Latin America	120	125	126	128	133	102	103	100	99	100
Near East	122	124	128	138	131	104	103	102	107	98
Asian centrally planned economies	116	122	125	123	128	104	107	108	105	107
Total developing countries	118	123	125	125	129	103	105	104	101	102
World	118	122	126	126	131	105	106	108	106	108

[a] Including countries in other regions not specified.

Source: World Food Conference, *Assessment of the World Food Situation*, Table 1.

Table 5

INDICES OF TOTAL AND PER CAPITA FOOD AND AGRICULTURAL PRODUCTION IN WORLD AND VARIOUS REGIONS (USDA DATA), 1969–73

(index numbers, 1961–65 average = 100)

Area	Total					Per Capita				
	1969	1970	1971	1972	1973	1969	1970	1971	1972	1973
	Food Production									
World [a]	118	121	126	124	123	105	106	108	104	110
Developed countries	117	119	125	124	133	121	126	128	125	132
Developing countries [a]	121	126	128	125	132	104	106	105	100	103
	Agricultural Production									
World [a]	117	120	125	123	130	104	105	107	104	108
Developed countries	116	118	123	122	129	109	110	114	112	117
Developing countries [a]	120	124	127	125	131	103	104	104	100	102
Regions										
United States	110	109	118	118	120					
Canada	128	112	129	120	123					
Latin America	118	122	126	125	132					
Western Europe	112	113	120	119	121					
Eastern Europe	119	116	122	132	135					
U.S.S.R.	123	136	135	129	154					
South Asia	119	126	127	119	130					
West Asia	122	124	131	138	127					
Other East Asia [b]	124	130	134	132	144					
Africa [c]	118	117	120	123	120					
Oceania	121	119	123	116	118					

[a] Excludes Communist Asia.
[b] Excludes Japan.
[c] Excludes South Africa.

Source: Food production from Table 2 above, p. 16; agricultural production from Economic Research Service, *World Agricultural Situation*, WAS-6, December 1974, p. 5.

Table 6

WORLD GRAIN PRODUCTION AND CONSUMPTION WITH
TREND ESTIMATES, 1969/70 THROUGH 1974/75

(million metric tons)

Year	Grain Production			Grain Consumption		
	Actual	Trend [a]	Deviation	Actual	Trend [a]	Deviation
1969/70–1971/72	1,059	1,056	+ 3	1,068	1,066	+ 2
1971/72	1,116	1,085	+31	1,097	1,096	+ 1
1972/73	1,083	1,114	−31	1,131	1,126	+ 5
1973/74	1,182	1,143	+38	1,180	1,155	+25
1974/75	1,122	1,172	−50	1,148	1,185	−37

[a] Trend is for the years 1960–73.

Source: Economic Research Service, *World Agricultural Situation*, WAS-6, December 1974, p. 27.

world are known to have been increasing at about 2.8 percent annually since 1960 (along with the annual 2 percent growth in population).

Grain production was above trend production by 31 million tons in 1971/72, below trend by 31 million tons in 1972/73. The actual decline in grain production between the two years was only 33 million tons, or about 3 percent. Based on past experience, we would have expected an increase in production of about 30 million tons in the two years, assuming normal growing conditions in each year. However, production was unusually high in 1971/72 and unusually low in 1972/73.

The data on estimated world grain consumption throws a somewhat different light on the degree of food stringency for the world in 1972/73. According to these estimates, world grain consumption actually increased between 1971/72 and 1972/73 and by somewhat more than the trend amount. The actual increase was 34 million tons, while the trend increase was 30 million tons. Thus, if the estimates are accurate, enough grain was available in 1972/73 to maintain world per capita consumption at a rate equal to that of 1971/72, and it was indeed maintained. Obviously, averages tell us nothing about the actual distribution of grain consumption among regions and countries. Later in this chapter, data on changes in the distribution of available grain supplies between the two years will be presented. The increase in world grain consumption between

1971/72 and 1972/73 was made possible by a decline in world grain stocks. Grain stocks declined by about 41 million tons during 1972/73.[3]

Grain, of course, is not a homogeneous commodity. Wheat and rice are primarily food grains, while a significant fraction—much more than half—of the production of corn, barley, oats, sorghums, and millets is used as feed. Thus, if there had been a significant shift in the kinds of grain produced and consumed between 1971/72 and 1972/73, the world totals would be subject to misinterpretation. However, the percentage declines in production between the two years for wheat, rice, and the coarse grains were quite similar—2.2 percent, 3.4 percent, and 2.0 percent, respectively. Of the three grains, only rice consumption actually declined and by 2 percent. Wheat consumption increased by 6.5 percent and coarse grain consumption by 4.5 percent; total grain consumption increased by 3.9 percent.[4] Thus, it does not appear that there were significant changes in production or consumption between the food grains and the coarse grains between the two years.

The data in Table 6 indicate that 1973/74 was a year of record grain production and consumption, while 1974/75 was a relatively poor year, with production almost 4 percent below trend and consumption 3 percent below trend.

Peruvian Anchovies

For reasons not fully understood, the catch of anchovies off the coast of Peru declined substantially between 1972 and 1973. But the supply and price effects of the decline on Peruvian fish meal production could be and probably have been overestimated, although, of course, the decline remains another piece of "bad news" with respect to feed and food supplies. The decline in Peruvian production of fish meal from 1972 to 1973 was equivalent to 750,000 tons of soybean meal.[5] Estimated world production of all oil meals, including fish meal, was 63.7 million tons in 1972; the total was 63.6 million tons for 1973.[6] Thus, the decline in Peruvian fish meal production was

[3] Ibid., p. 22. The stock data are for wheat and feed grains and thus exclude rice. Rice stocks are much less important quantitatively than wheat and feed grain stocks.

[4] Economic Research Service, U.S. Department of Agriculture, *World Agricultural Situation*, WAS-6, December 1974, pp. 28, 32-34. Revised and comparable data for 1971/72 were supplied by the Economic Research Service.

[5] Ibid., WAS-4, December 1973, p. 32.

[6] Ibid., WAS-6, p. 38.

only a little more than 1 percent of world production of oil meals. In 1974 oil meal production increased substantially to 74.5 million tons.

Soviet Grain Purchases

In the summer of 1972, the Soviet Union made enormous purchases of grains from the rest of the world, a large fraction being the much publicized and highly subsidized wheat purchase from the United States. This is not the place to discuss most aspects of these transactions; relatively good analyses may be found elsewhere.[7] What is relevant for our purposes is the effect of the Russian imports upon world food supplies and prices.

In 1972/73 the Soviet Union imported 20.5 million tons of grain, of which 14.9 million tons were wheat. During the same year, it is estimated that the Soviet Union exported 1.3 million tons of wheat and 0.2 million tons of feed grains, producing a net import position of 19 million tons. In the previous year, 1971/72, 7.7 million tons had been imported, of which 4.3 million tons were feed grains—the first year of significant feed grain imports. Net grain imports in that year, however, were only 1.2 million tons since exports totaled 6.5 million tons. In 1970/71 the Soviet Union had been a significant net grain exporter, with net exports of 7.3 million tons, but in 1973/74, even with a bumper grain crop, it was a small net importer, with net grain imports of 3.6 million tons.[8]

The Soviet Union was also a significant grain importer in 1963/64 (10.4 million tons, gross) and in 1965/66 (9.0 million tons, gross). The U.S.S.R.'s earlier excursions into the international market differed significantly from that of 1972/73. Between 1962/63 and 1963/64 Soviet grain production, according to official estimates, declined by almost 33 million tons; between 1964/65 and 1965/66 the decline was 31 million tons. Increased gross imports equaled

---

[7] Clifton B. Luttrell, "The Russian Wheat Deal—Hindsight vs. Foresight," *St. Louis Federal Reserve Bank Bulletin*, October 1973, pp. 2-9. Mr. Luttrell argues convincingly that most of the adverse reaction to the wheat and corn sale was the result of hindsight: "In September 1972, few observable indicators pointed to the short world supply of key farm products and the sharp price increases that subsequently occurred. No widely distributed forecast indicated price increases of 140 percent for wheat, 165 percent for corn and 210 percent for soybeans by August 1973" (pp. 3-4).

[8] Hathaway, "Food Prices and Inflation," p. 89, for data on imports and exports of wheat and feed grains by the Soviet Union; and Economic Research Service, *World Agricultural Situation*, WAS-6, December 1974, p. 28, for data on grain production.

less than a third of the declines in output. The 1972/73 grain crop was only 13 million tons below the previous year, and yet net grain imports increased by almost 18 million tons.[9] In effect, a significant change in policy had occurred between the mid-1960s and 1972/73. In the earlier period, apparently, the government imported the amount of grain required to prevent famine or at least a very sharp reduction in the food use of grain. Livestock herds, especially hogs, were allowed to decline substantially as a result of reduced feed supplies.[10] In the early 1970s, on the other hand, the Soviet Union apparently decided that such a reduction in livestock herds and production of livestock products was to be avoided in the future. To some degree, this decision was signaled to the world in 1971/72 when substantial feed grain was imported even though that year's crop was the second highest on record.[11]

The major grain exporters did not foresee that the U.S.S.R.'s actual net grain imports would be larger than the decline in production. And it is hard to fault either the private trade or governmental agencies for this forecasting error. Another reason for the forecasting error was the assumption that the Soviet Union would have accumulated significant stocks of grain from the two bumper grain crops of 1970 and 1971. To have done so would have represented rational behavior in a market economy, but the Soviet Union is not a market economy. Subsequent analysis seems to indicate that instead of increasing grain stocks the U.S.S.R. actually reduced them during the two bumper years.[12]

Some perspective on the significance of the Soviet grain imports can be obtained by comparisons with total world grain exports for

---

[9] David M. Schoonover, "The Soviet Feed-Livestock Economy: Preliminary Findings on Performance and Trade Implications," in Economic Research Service, U.S. Department of Agriculture, *Prospects for Agricultural Trade with the USSR*, ERS-Foreign 356, April 1974, p. 30.

[10] D. Gale Johnson, "The Soviet Livestock Sector: Problems and Prospects," *Association for Comparative Economic Studies Bulletin*, vol. 16, no. 2 (Fall 1974), p. 41. The number of hogs declined from 70 million at the beginning of 1963 to 41 million at the end, and it was not until 1972 that the swine herd returned to the level of January 1963.

[11] D. Gale Johnson, "Soviet Agriculture and World Trade in Farm Products," in Economic Research Service, *Prospects for Agricultural Trade with the USSR*, p. 44. At the 1972 Agricultural Outlook Conference, February 23, 1972, I noted that following the excellent grain crops in 1970 and 1971 (the two largest Soviet crops on record up to that time) the Soviet Union imported about 5 million tons of grain. The shift in priorities may well have occurred not in 1972 but at least a year earlier, and the implications of that shift appear to have been missed by outsiders generally, including this writer.

[12] Schoonover, "The Soviet Feed-Livestock Economy," p. 30.

Table 7

WORLD EXPORTS OF WHEAT AND COARSE GRAINS AND
NET IMPORTS BY THE U.S.S.R., 1970/71 THROUGH 1974/75

(million metric tons)

Year	World Wheat Exports	U.S.S.R. Net Wheat Imports [a]	World Coarse Grain Exports	U.S.S.R. Net Coarse Grain Imports [a]
1970/71	56.2	+ 6.7	52.6	+0.6
1971/72	56.0	+ 2.4	56.1	3.6
1972/73	73.1	13.6	64.6	6.0
1973/74	68.7	+ 0.6	76.7	5.0
1974/75 [b]	67.9	+ 4.0	57.2	0.5

[a] A plus sign means net exports.

[b] Forecast.

Sources: Foreign Agriculture Service, U.S. Department of Agriculture, *Foreign Agriculture Circular*, March 1974; and Economic Research Service, *World Agricultural Situation*, WAS-5, September 1974, p. 31, and WAS-6, December 1974, pp. 32-33.

recent years. As indicated in Table 7, the 16 million ton increase in net wheat imports by the Soviet Union between 1971/72 and 1972/73 accounted for nearly all of the increase in world wheat exports between the two years. For the next two years, however, the Soviet Union was a net exporter (or is anticipated to be, since the data for 1974/75 represent a forecast). Thus, in only one of three years of substantially increased world wheat exports did the Soviet Union's imports account for an important part of the increase.

An additional insight into the significance of the U.S. sales of grain to the Soviet Union may be obtained by comparing the total value of exports of agricultural products from the United States with the value of exports to the Soviet Union for the year prior to the grain sales and the next two years. Total agricultural exports from the United States were valued at $8.047 billion in 1971/72, at $12.901 billion in 1972/73, and at $21.320 billion in 1973/74. U.S. exports of agricultural products to the Soviet Union were $135 million, $900 million, and $509 million, respectively. Thus, of the increase in total exports of $4.850 billion from 1971/72 to 1972/73, exports to the Soviet Union accounted for about 16 percent, and of the increase between 1971/72 and 1973/74, exports to the Soviet Union accounted for less than 4 percent.[13]

Increased Affluence and Recent Developments

In Chapter 4 I shall consider the effects of affluence on the longer-run food supply of the poorer people of the world. But at the moment the question is whether increased affluence was in some way responsible for the food difficulties of 1973 and 1974. The authors of the two quotations given below clearly believe it was.

> A major factor in the price increases [since 1971] has been the demand for grains and other sources of concentrated livestock feed generated by the growing demand for live-stock products.[14]
>
> The various explanations of the current crisis embody a combination of factors that culminated in a "flash point" in world grain prices. First, and in my view, most important has been the long-run growth in demand for feed grains and oilseeds resulting from the spreading affluence in both the developed and developing world.[15]

The first quotation is from the excellent *Assessment of the World Food Situation, Present and Future,* prepared for the 1974 World Food Conference. The second is a comment in the same vein from an outstanding agricultural economist, Dale E. Hathaway.

As is well known, and correctly noted by Hathaway elsewhere in the article I have quoted, increasing per capita incomes in the industrial or developed countries have little or no effect on the per capita consumption of food grains—wheat and rice. The effect instead is felt in increased per capita consumption of livestock products.[16] The question, then, is whether the rate of growth in the demand for livestock products and feed has outrun productions and supplies of feed, presumably with the crossover coming in the period from 1970 through 1972.

Between 1960–62 and 1969–71 the developed market economies increased their per capita grain use for all purposes 13.9 percent, or at an annual compound rate of 1.4 percent. Between 1964–66 and

[13] Economic Research Service, U.S. Department of Agriculture, *FATUS: Foreign Agricultural Trade of the United States,* August 1973, p. 8, and August 1974, p. 7.
[14] World Food Conference, *Assessment of the World Food Situation,* p. 21.
[15] Hathaway, "Food Prices and Inflation," p. 95.
[16] Ibid., pp. 90-91.

1972/73 (the period considered by Hathaway) the increase in per capita use was 14.7 percent, for an annual rate of 1.9 percent.[17]

The increases in grain use among the developed market economies were smaller than the increases in grain production since 1960–62. As a result, net grain exports to the rest of the world rose from 20.3 million tons in 1960–62 to 31.9 million tons in 1969–71 and to somewhat more than 60 million tons on average for 1972/73 and 1973/74.[18] Thus, if affluence is charged with the increasing per capita use of grain, it should also be credited with increasing per capita production of grain. On balance, the developed market economies added more to production than to consumption.

It is true that, over the same period, some of the developed countries—the Soviet Union and Eastern Europe—increased their grain use somewhat more than their grain production. From 1960–62 through 1969–71, per capita grain consumption in the Soviet Union and Eastern Europe increased by 22.9 percent, while per capita grain production increased by 21.3 percent. These increases represent annual growth rates of 2.3 and 2.2 percent. There was a sharp increase in per capita grain use in 1972/73 and 1973/74 that was not fully compensated by increased production. If per capita consumption is averaged for these two years, the increase from 1960–62 was 43.5 percent, for an annual rate of growth of 3.2 percent. Production per capita increased by 34.1 percent (2.3 percent annually).[19] There was no sudden jump in per capita income or affluence in the Soviet Union that would explain the rapid growth in per capita consumption. Thus it is difficult to attribute the change in consumption in 1972/73 and 1973/74 to affluence; rather, the increase must be the result of a deliberate policy change.

If we do not separate out the Soviet Union and Eastern Europe but combine all of the high-income countries, production will be found to have increased somewhat more than consumption between 1960–62 and 1969–71 or 1972/73. Net exports to the rest of the world were 20.8 million tons in 1960–62, 29.7 million tons in 1969–71, and almost 42 million tons in 1972/73.[20]

---

[17] Economic Research Service, *World Agricultural Situation*, WAS-4, December 1973, p. 23; WAS-5, September 1974, p. 27; and WAS-6, December 1974, p. 28. Calculations of per capita use of grain were made by the author for 1960-62, 1969-71, and 1972/73 from population data supplied by the Economic Research Service.

[18] For sources, see n. 17, above.

[19] Ibid.

[20] Ibid. In the estimates of net trade in grain, there is a substantial volume of exports left unaccounted for, which must be treated as a statistical discrepancy. Data on exports are probably more accurate than data on imports. However,

One further point concerning grain production in the developed countries needs to be made. As noted in Chapter 2, the three major wheat exporters deliberately and drastically reduced wheat production between 1968 and 1970—from 75.4 million tons to 54.2 million tons. From the beginning of 1968 to the beginning of 1970, wheat stocks in the three countries—Australia, Canada, and the United States—increased from 34.2 million tons to 58.9 million tons, and a conscious effort was made to reduce the stocks in order to raise wheat prices since there seemed to be no immediate prospect for increased demand to absorb some of the stocks.[21]

There is no evidence of a sudden upsurge in meat production and consumption in the developed countries that could explain the sharp increase in grain prices after 1972. Estimates of annual beef and pork production in countries that produce approximately 75 percent of the world's total indicate that the production of these two meats increased by only 8 percent between 1968 and 1972—from 42.0 million tons to 45.4 million tons.[22] Meat production fell in 1973, contributing to the sharp increase in meat prices during that year, but then recovered in 1974 and meat prices declined significantly from their 1973 peaks.[23]

It should be noted, however, that, while meat production in the industrial countries increased only moderately during the early 1970s, there was a significant increase in livestock numbers, especially cattle, which added to the demand for feed from 1971 through 1973.[24] The increase in cattle numbers should have had a greater effect on the demand for nongrain feed than on grain, even though there was a positive effect on grain.

---

data on net known grain imports of the developing countries, including China, may be of interest: 1960-62, 14.0 million tons; 1969-71, 22.4 million tons, and 1972/73, 32.5 million tons. The basic conclusion remains the same—the developed countries did not increase consumption by more than their available supplies.

[21] Data on wheat stocks from Economic Research Service, *World Agricultural Situation*, WAS-2, November 1971, p. 10.

[22] Ibid., WAS-4, December 1973, p. 35. Two countries usually classified as developing countries were included in the production data—Argentina and Brazil. Their combined production amounted to about 10 percent of the total for the selected countries. The exclusion of Argentina and Brazil from the total does not change the percentage increase in pork and beef production. These data indicate that, for the industrial countries, per capita consumption of beef and pork increased only 1 percent annually from 1968 to 1972—hardly a high or an unusual increase.

[23] "World commercial meat production is growing again in 1974, reversing the sharp 1973 drop." Economic Research Service, *World Agricultural Situation*, WAS-5, September 1974, p. 42.

[24] Ibid., WAS-4, December 1973, p. 37.

Effect of the Business Cycle

There was almost certainly a cyclical element in the 1973 price increases for grains and other food products. According to available evidence, there was a definite slowdown in world economic growth from 1969 through the beginning of 1971 and then a rather rapid recovery extending through 1973. Based on FAO estimates of the income elasticities of demand for food products at the farm level, the growth in per capita demand for the world in the 1960s was about 0.7 percent annually, falling to about 0.55 percent in 1971 and increasing to 0.8 percent in 1972 and 1.0 percent in 1973.[25] If we assume a price elasticity of demand for food at the farm level of −0.05 and a completely inelastic supply of food, the maximum increase in prices at the farm level would have been less than 36 percent between 1971 and 1973. More realistically, we might have expected at most a 20 percent increase in farm prices—assuming reasonable freedom for market forces to work—as a result of the cyclical change in economic growth.

Governmental Price Policies

The decline in grain production relative to trend production was not large enough to explain the increase in grain prices. Nor does the increase in meat production that occurred in 1972 and 1973 seem large enough to have had more than a minimal effect. The decline in fish meal production also had a small effect, but only that. Thus, while changes in underlying supply and demand relations could have increased grain prices somewhat, it is difficult to see how the increase could have been greater than 50 percent. If we add another 15 percent for the effects of the overvaluation of the dollar, there still remains a substantial and unexplained residual.

I believe that the residual increase can be explained only by the price policies followed by governments in several large countries. It must be remembered that the price increases of 100 to 200 percent from mid-1972 to 1974 occurred in a particular market—in the export markets for wheat, feed grains, and rice. These increases were reflected in the domestic prices of relatively few of the industrial countries, principally in the United States, Canada, and Australia. If one could calculate a weighted average of grain prices received by

---

[25] Economic Research Service, *The World Food Situation*, pp. 76-77.

producers or paid by consumers of grain, the increases would have been much smaller than the export price increases.

In the countries that consume approximately half of the world's grain, price increases have been small since 1971/72, and in a number of instances real prices of grain have declined. In these countries, there has been no incentive for either producers or consumers to react to the changes in the demand and supply situation for grain that occurred in 1972/73 and subsequently. Virtually all of the response to the small reductions in production occurred in a limited sector of the world's segmented market for grain.

In the original six countries of the Common Market, grain prices received by farmers in national currencies in mid-1974 were at most 20 percent above the 1971/72 levels in all countries except Italy, where the increase was about 40 percent.[26] This means that there were declines in the real prices received by producers. There have been no announced farm price increases for grains in the Soviet Union, at least none that have come to my attention.

In effect, a large part of the world has not shared the consequences of the modest production shortfalls of 1972 through 1974. Thus, we should not be surprised when grain prices in those markets that are relatively open rise very substantially. Virtually all of the difference between supply and demand at the pre-1972 prices in those countries that have not permitted prices to increase has found its way into the international market. Prior to 1972/73, only 10 percent of the world's grain moved in international trade. It is this market that has been forced to adjust to the difference between supply and demand in the world as a whole. The international market could have absorbed the production shortfalls with a rather modest increase in prices if producers and consumers in all nations had been given the proper price signals. But such was not the case. As a consequence, consumers in many developing countries and in the major exporting nations were forced to pay much higher prices for grain products than those in nations whose governments insulated them from the effects of production variability.

---

[26] Food and Agriculture Organization, *Monthly Bulletin of Agricultural Economics and Statistics*, September 1974, pp. 48-56; and Canada Department of Agriculture, *Agriculture Abroad*, vol. 29, no. 4 (August 1974), pp. 30-31.

4

INCREASING AFFLUENCE
AS A THREAT TO THE POOR

Chapter 3 dealt with the hypothesis that affluence is responsible, at least in part, for the sharp increase in grain and other farm prices since 1971/72. The conclusion was that the concurrent economic recovery in the developed market economies that started in 1970 could have had a modest effect upon numbers of livestock and thus upon grain prices but that the increases could not have amounted to more than 20 percent and probably would have been closer to 10 percent. Pork and beef production in the major producing areas rose by only 8 percent between 1968 and 1972 and actually declined in 1973. It was unfortunate that the buildup in cattle herds continued for at least two years after the reduction in grain production in 1972, but this was more a reflection of errors in expectations than of increasing affluence.

Running through many discussions of the world food situation is the view that affluence—high incomes—constitutes a threat to the poor people of the world. The argument has taken two forms. One is the view that the high-income countries should reduce their food consumption, especially meat, in order to build up grain reserves.[1] The other is concerned with our longer-run responsibilities for the world food situation. It is pointed out that in the United States we consume approximately 2,000 pounds of grain per person per year

---

[1] Lester R. Brown, in his testimony before the Senate Subcommittees on Agricultural Production, Marketing, and Stabilization of Prices and on Foreign Agricultural Policy of the Committee on Agriculture and Forestry, stated: "Given the precariousness of the world food balance at present it might be wise to reduce consumption of meat a few pounds per capita within affluent, overnourished societies such as the United States in order to accumulate some food reserves now to lessen the chaos which will result a year hence if the drought cycle should return to North America next year" (*Hearings on U.S. and World Food Situation*, 93rd Cong., 1st sess., October 1973, p. 103).

compared with about 400 pounds in many developing countries. Thus, one American makes as large a demand upon the world's grain supplies as five Indians or Chinese or Pakistanis. It is also stated that increased per capita incomes in the United States and other industrial countries result in higher per capita consumption of livestock products and an important increase in per capita use of grain.[2] From these correct or almost correct statements, the conclusion is reached or implied that the consumption patterns of the high-income countries reduce the amount of grain available to the poor countries of the world. Such a conclusion is largely irrelevant to the task of improving the food situation of the poor people of the world.

Before the high-income countries significantly reduce their consumption of grain by reducing their consumption of livestock products, we need to consider what the longer-run effects would have been if such reductions had occurred in the past. Suppose that the United States and the other industrial countries had held their direct and indirect per capita use of grain to half of the actual levels for the past several decades. Would this have made more food available to India or Pakistan in 1973 and 1974? The answer is clearly no. The United States, and the other industrial countries as well, would have produced much less grain than has been produced. Reserve stocks would have been much smaller than they have been. If U.S. grain production in 1972 had been 125 million metric tons instead of 200 million or more, it would not have been politically possible to have had 70 million metric tons of grain reserves. Nor would Canada, with much lower export demand from the other industrial countries, have held such large stocks of grain in recent years. It might also be noted that, if the industrial countries had had much lower total grain consumption in the past, the institutions required to handle the grain exports to the developing countries in the mid-1960s or in 1972/73 and 1973/74 would not have been able to do so. International trade in grains would have virtually disappeared. Western Europe would not have required grain imports, even with a much smaller reduction in grain consumption than postulated here.

Even with the actual—or as some would say, excessive—grain consumption in the industrial countries in recent years, grain pro-

[2] At the hearing referred to in n. 1, above, Lester Brown said: "Throughout the world, per capita grain requirements, both direct and indirect, rise with income. The amount of grain consumed directly rises until per capita income approaches $500 a year, whereupon it begins to decline, eventually leveling off at about 150 pounds. The total amount of grain consumed directly and indirectly climbs. As yet no nation appears to have reached a level of affluence where its per capita grain requirements have stopped rising" (ibid., p. 88). See also the later section with the heading "Competition between Rich and Poor" (p. 99).

duction was below potential output level in the late 1960s and early 1970s. There is a fundamental and necessary relationship between demand and supply for a given product or group of products. Policy suggestions or recommendations that ignore this relationship can do great damage to human welfare.

It might be argued that the potential for expanding grain production in 1974 and 1975 would have been much greater with a lower output level. But this does not follow either. How much would have been spent on corn research over the past two decades if our annual production had been 3 billion bushels or less? And if there had been little prospect for increased demand? Would the major breakthroughs that cut the cost of nitrogen fertilizer almost in half in the early 1960s have occurred if grain production in the industrial countries had been half of the existing level? It is simply not possible to change a single major variable, such as per capita grain utilization, by a large fraction and then assume that everything else will remain the same.

Nor does it follow that, if per capita grain utilization in the industrial countries had been substantially lower, grain prices would also have been lower in recent years than they were. In other words, it cannot be assumed that the developing countries would have been able to buy grain in international markets at lower prices. Real grain prices and costs have fallen for the past six decades. This has occurred at the same time that output has increased substantially. Incentives for the development of new production techniques have both reduced costs and made possible greater output. If instead demand for grain had nearly stagnated in the industrial countries as population growth rates declined, incentives for investment in research and development would have been much more limited.

It was noted earlier that the total per capita utilization of grain in the United States was very high, about five times the per capita consumption in many developing countries. This high per capita consumption of grain, both directly and indirectly through livestock products, is generally attributed to our high and increasing per capita incomes. Between 1909 and 1971 the per capita gross national product in the United States increased by 180 percent. And yet per capita grain utilization in the United States actually declined between 1909 and 1971.

Table 8 presents data on the quantities of grain and all concentrates fed to livestock, total and per capita, and the direct per capita use of grain as food. The data in the table do not exhaust the total domestic use of grain; they do not include its use as seed, for

Table 8

TOTAL AND PER CAPITA USE OF GRAIN AND FEED CONCENTRATES BY LIVESTOCK AND PER CAPITA HUMAN USE OF GRAIN IN THE UNITED STATES, SELECTED YEARS

Year	Population (millions)	Total Use by Livestock		Per Capita Use				
		Grain (million metric tons)	All concentrates	Livestock			Total	
				Human	Grain	Concentrates (kilograms per year)	Grain	Concentrates
1909	90.5	72.2	86.6	136	798	956	934	1,092
1929	121.5	77.4	96.8	107	637	797	744	904
1939	130.6	75.6	93.9	91	563	719	654	810
1950	151.1	90.6	119.2	76	599	788	675	864
1960	180.0	113.1	138.6	67	628	770	695	837
1971	206.5	145.9	176.7	64	706	856	770	920

Sources: Ralph D. Jennings, *Consumption of Feed by Livestock, 1909–56*, USDA Production Research Report, no. 21, November 1958, pp. 82, 92; George C. Allen and Earl F. Hodges, *Livestock-Feed Relationships—National and State*, USDA Statistical Bulletin, no. 530, June 1974, p. 175. Direct per capita grain consumption is from USDA, *Agricultural Statistics*, various issues.

alcoholic beverages, and for other limited industrial products such as starch. The exclusion of alcoholic beverages results in the omission of about 4 million tons of grain utilization in 1970.[3]

The per capita use of grain feed and direct human use of grain declined substantially from 1909 to 1939, and the primary reason for this decline was the substitution of mechanical power for animal power. This substitution was essentially completed by 1950. Between 1950 and 1971, per capita grain use increased by only 14 percent, or 0.6 percent annually.

Data on all concentrates fed to livestock have been included in Table 8 since many of the nongrain concentrates, especially the oil meals, are close substitutes for grain in production. For completeness, by-products from the food industry are also included since livestock consume several million tons. However, changes in per capita use over time are essentially the same, whether it is of grain or of all concentrates. Per capita use of grain declined by 18 percent between 1909 and 1971, and per capita use of all concentrates declined by 16 percent.

Some who read an earlier presentation of the material in Table 8 argued that a comparison made over such a long period of time is largely irrelevant. Obviously, there cannot be a second replacement of animal power by tractors, and no such implication was intended. But there is a high positive correlation between tractor use and per capita gross national product. As per capita incomes increase elsewhere, similar substitutions will be occurring, as they have in Western Europe and Japan over the past two decades.

If one excludes the concentrates fed to horses and mules in 1909, per capita use of all concentrates for direct use and feeding to livestock other than horses and mules was 824 kilograms. Over six decades to 1971 per capita use of concentrates for food increased only 11 percent! Over the same period of time, per capita consumption of animal products increased by 20 percent.[4]

As remarked earlier, before we enter upon campaigns to shame people in the industrial countries into reducing their food consumption, we should be certain that such a reduction would in fact improve the situation in the developing countries. We should get the facts straight. Father Hesburgh, chairman of the Overseas Development

---

[3] Economic Research Service, U.S. Department of Agriculture, *Feed Statistics,* Supplement for 1971 to Statistical Bulletin, no. 410, July 1972, p. 14.

[4] Economic Research Service, U.S. Department of Agriculture, *Food Consumption, Prices, and Expenditures,* Supplement for 1972 to Agricultural Economic Report, no. 138, p. 9.

Council, has told us that if each American ate one less McDonald's hamburger each week, we would save 10 million tons of grain for the developing countries.[5] This is definitely wrong. Much of the hamburger meat in the United States is derived from Australian grass-fed beef and discarded dairy and beef cows; thus, the grain content of hamburger meat is quite low. Father Hesburgh should have suggested eating fewer steaks and prime rib roasts since the grain saving for these products would be substantial.

There is a considerable amount of misunderstanding and misinformation about the extent to which the use of grain in the production of beef and the direct human use of grain are competitive. In a generally good review of the world food situation, *Time* stated the following: "The industrial world's way of eating is an extremely inefficient use of resources. For every pound of beef consumed, a steer has gobbled 20 pounds of grain."[6] No source was given and none could be given since the amount of grain mentioned as necessary to produce a pound of beef was simply wrong.

The estimated feed requirements per 100 pounds of beef produced (liveweight) in 1970 was 1,054 pounds of feed units.[7] The feed unit represents the feed value of a pound of corn. Since the ratio of meat to liveweight for beef is approximately one-half, the amount of feed per pound of meat would be approximately twenty pounds. Such a calculation may have been the basis for the statement made by *Time*. However, beef cattle consume feed other than grains. In 1970, of the estimated total feed units fed to beef cattle, only

[5] William Hines, writing in the Chicago *Sun-Times* (April 14, 1974, section 1-A, p. 4), summarized the speech in which Father Hesburgh suggested that Americans eat one less McDonald's "Quarter-Pounder" hamburger each week. A simple calculation indicates that such an action would reduce the consumption of hamburgers by 10 billion annually. The saving in grain was to come from both the beef and the bun, but since the buns would not weigh more than 1 million tons, most of the saving would have to come from the grain that would have been used to produce the beef. Father Hesburgh's suggestion that Americans eat 10 billion fewer hamburgers per year aroused my curiosity about the number of hamburgers sold annually by all drive-ins in the United States. A survey of separate eating places made by the U.S. Department of Agriculture in 1969 indicates the probable upper limit. If an average hamburger contains one-tenth of a pound (not the one-quarter pound referred to by Father Hesburgh), the total number of hamburgers sold at McDonald's and similar establishments was about 4 billion in 1969. An estimate based on the number of hamburger buns leads to approximately the same figure. If Father Hesburgh's suggestion had been followed, McDonald's and all similar establishments would have been forced to close. My estimate of the number of hamburgers sold is based on data from Michael G. Van Dress, *Separate Eating Places: Type, Quantity and Value of Foods Used*, USDA Statistical Bulletin, no. 487, June 1972, pp. 17, 20.

[6] *Time*, November 11, 1974, p. 75.

[7] U.S. Department of Agriculture, *Agricultural Statistics, 1972*, p. 425.

Table 9

PER CAPITA USE OF GRAIN IN DEVELOPED MARKET
ECONOMIES, THE UNITED STATES, EASTERN EUROPE
AND THE SOVIET UNION, SELECTED YEARS

(kilograms per year)

Years	Developed Market Economies [a]	United States	Eastern Europe and Soviet Union
1960–62	465 [b]	757	534
1964–66	482	743	601
1969–71	530	723	680
1971–73	543	852	732
1974–75	510	723	749

[a] Includes the United States.

[b] Each of the figures is an average of three years; for example, those for 1960–62 are based on 1960/61, 1961/62, and 1962/63. Data for 1974/75 are projections made by Economic Research Service, U.S. Department of Agriculture.

Sources: Consumption data are from Economic Research Service, *World Agricultural Situation*, WAS-4, December 1973; WAS-5, September 1974; and WAS-6, December 1974. Population data are from Food and Agriculture Organization, *Production Yearbook*, various issues.

22 percent consisted of grains and only 26 percent consisted of concentrates. Approximately 56 percent of all feed for beef cattle is pasturage.[8] The much-criticized feedlot production of beef accounts for only 28 percent of the total feed fed to beef cattle. *Time* would have been more accurate if it had said that four or five pounds of grain were required for each pound of beef consumed.

Much has been made of the high annual rate of grain consumption in the industrial countries. What is seldom noted is that, except for Eastern Europe and the Soviet Union, the growth in per capita grain use in the industrial countries has been very modest since 1960. Table 9 gives data on the per capita use of grain in selected years for all of the developed market economies, for the United States, and for Eastern Europe and the Soviet Union. All of the developed market economies, including the United States, increased their per capita grain use by 17 percent between 1960–62 and 1971–73. This is an annual rate of growth of only 1.4 percent. Grain use in the United States increased somewhat less—12.5 percent, for an annual rate of

[8] George C. Allen and Earl F. Hodges, *Livestock-Feed Relationships—National and State*, USDA Statistical Bulletin, no. 530, June 1974, p. 178.

1.1 percent. The increase in per capita grain use in Eastern Europe was much greater—37.2 percent overall and 2.9 percent annually. But this was due less to an increase in affluence than to policy changes that gave greater recognition to consumer preferences.

The high rate of per capita use of grains in the industrial countries does provide a reserve that can be drawn upon, if the price system is permitted to work. The feed use of grain can and will be reduced if the price relationships between livestock products and grain encourage it. As of December 1974, it was projected that world grain use in 1974/75 would be 32 million tons below 1973/74. Of this total reduction, 25 million tons was projected to occur in the United States. All of the reduction was to occur as a result of reduced feeding of grain to livestock.

The projected per capita use of grain in the United States in 1974/75 is below per capita use in 1960–62 (see Table 9). This expected reduction is not the result of a decline in meat consumption, which for consumption is being maintained by a reduction in the rate of growth of the beef cattle herd. Increased beef supplies are more than offsetting reductions in pork and poultry supplies.

Unfortunately, the other high-income countries, except Canada and Australia, have not permitted prices to ration available supplies and reduce feed use of grain. In the European Economic Community, in the rest of Western Europe, and in Japan, grain use is projected to be 11 million tons more in 1974/75 than in 1971/72. In Eastern Europe and the Soviet Union, the increase in grain use is projected to be even larger, 22 million tons.

The effects of affluence on food must be viewed in terms of total effects, not just the effects on demand. Affluence, or relatively high per capita incomes, is associated with a variety of factors that result in relatively high output of food per unit of land, capital, and labor. By considering only the effects of affluence upon the absolute level of demand, we are likely to make mistakes that will harm the world's poor people rather than help them.

5
ARE HIGH FARM PRICES HERE TO STAY?

A short answer to the question posed by the title to this chapter is, Not for very long. I see nothing in the events of 1973 and 1974 that will result in a significant reversal of the long-run trend toward lower grain prices. In fact, if the analysis in Chapter 3 is roughly correct in placing much of the responsibility for the substantial increases in international grain prices upon the policy actions of governments, the declines in grain prices could be as abrupt and as drastic as the increases have been. Since the restraints upon adjustment to modest shortfalls in production will also operate to prevent adjustments when production returns to or exceeds trend levels, virtually all of the price impact of the new situation will be imposed upon a limited part of the world's highly segmented markets for grain and many other food products.

There are others who see the recent and current relative stringency in food supplies as a permanent situation, with continually rising real costs of farm products as a definite possibility and a real threat to the health and welfare of the poorer people of the world.[1]

---

[1] A frequently quoted source of this view is Lester R. Brown. In a recent article, he summarized his position:

"This year's global food scarcity is often treated by both official Washington and the communications media as a temporary phenomenon, an aberration that will shortly disappear if we will only have patience. But several factors suggest that the world food economy is undergoing a fundamental transformation, and that food scarcity is becoming chronic.

"The soaring demand for food, spurred by continued population growth and rising affluence, has begun to outrun the productive capacity of the world's farmers and fishermen. The result has been declining food reserves, skyrocketing food prices, food rationing in three of the world's most populous countries, intense international competition for exportable food supplies, and export controls on major foodstuffs by the world's principal food supplier" (Brown, "The Next Crisis? Food," *Foreign Policy*, no. 13 [Winter 1973-74], p. 3).

This is the view expressed frequently in newspapers and national magazines and, as of the beginning of 1975, it is the popular view.

Those who say that the world will be faced with food prices substantially higher than those of the past decade have not, so far as I know, quantified such a prediction.[2] Are real food prices to be higher by 10 percent or 25 percent or 50 percent?

Depressed Grain Prices before 1972

There are grounds for believing that real grain prices in international markets will be somewhat higher in the future than during the four or five years prior to 1972. The primary reason is that international grain prices were depressed during that period by the overvaluation of the American dollar and, to a lesser extent, the Canadian dollar.[3] Increased imports of agricultural products by countries whose currencies have appreciated in terms of the dollar will result in higher grain prices for countries whose currencies are closely related to the dollar. To some considerable degree, the impact of the overvaluation of the dollar was offset for the American farmer by annual direct payments of $3 billion to $4 billion from 1968 through 1972.

But this source of increase in the international prices of grain— perhaps of the order of 10 to 15 percent in the long run—is not what the pessimists have in mind. As I understand their position, it is that the expansion of supply required to keep pace with the growth in demand will result in significantly higher unit costs of production for farm products. Such a development is possible, but is it likely? If it occurred, it would represent a reversal of a six-decade trend toward *lower* real prices of grain. Between 1910–14 and the 1971 crop year, the real farm price of feed grains and hay declined by 40 percent, and the real price of food declined by 37 percent. In both calculations, prices received have been adjusted to include direct government payments as though the total of such payments was a net addition to

---

2 "The international scarcity of major agricultural commodities which emerged in 1973 reflects important long term trends as well as the more temporary phenomenon of lack of rainfall in the Soviet Union and parts of Asia and Africa. We appear to be entering an extended period in which global grain reserves which provide a crucial measure of safety when crop failures occur, will generally remain on the low side, and in which little if any excess cropland will be held idle in the United States. Food prices are likely to remain considerably higher than they were during the last decade" (Lester R. Brown and Erik P. Eckholm, *U.S. and the Developing World* [Washington, D.C.: Overseas Development Council, 1974], p. 66).

3 G. Edward Schuh, "The Exchange Rate and U.S. Agriculture," *American Journal of Agricultural Economics*, vol. 56, no. 1 (February 1974), pp. 1-13.

prices and incomes.[4] The declines in real farm prices in the United States, as measured here, have been somewhat smaller than the declines in real export prices from the major grain exporting areas.[5]

Reasons Given for Higher Prices

Why is it expected that the real costs of producing grains will increase? The reasons appear to be the following: First, there is relatively little uncultivated land remaining, and all of the diverted acreage in the United States has been returned to production. Second, increasing yields will increase costs to some extent because of diminishing returns to fertilizer. And, third, the prices of farm inputs—especially those based on petroleum products—will be substantially higher in the future than in the past.[6]

The first two reasons given for rising real costs of grain are either incorrect or irrelevant or both. There are substantial possibilities for expanding the cultivated land area in Africa, South America, Southeast Asia, North America, and Australia.[7] It is true that the potential for expanding cultivated land in parts of Asia is relatively small, but this does not mean that the real costs of producing grains must inevitably increase. It is not at all certain that the cultivation of additional land is generally a significantly lower-cost means of expanding output than increasing yields per acre. The experience of the past several decades in the United States appears to show that it has generally been cheaper to expand output by increasing yields than by adding new land; some new land has been brought into cultiva-

---

[4] I have elsewhere argued that the direct payments did not increase net farm incomes by more than a third to a half of the gross payments received. See D. Gale Johnson, *Farm Commodity Programs: An Opportunity for Change* (Washington, D.C.: American Enterprise Institute, 1973), p. 48.

[5] Farm prices in the United States in 1971 included farm program payments and an export subsidy on wheat. No such distortions existed in 1910-14.

[6] Brown, "The Next Crisis?" pp. 7-10.

[7] "While in some developing countries the practical ceiling on land development may have been reached, in a large part of the developing world there remains land resources which are either unutilized or are utilized in production processes with very low returns. The largest 'land-reserves' in the developing countries are in South America, Africa and in parts of South East Asia. All of these regions suffer from specific limitations . . . but modern technology is increasingly able to cope with the problems and one may expect some very major development programmes for cultivated land in these regions" (World Food Conference, United Nations, *Assessment of the World Food Situation, Present and Future*, E/CONF. 65/3, 1974, p. 65). See also Chapter 8 for a further discussion.

tion, but far more has been retired.[8] It is clearly possible to increase yields in the developing countries. Although some increases have been achieved in the past three decades, yields are still much lower in the developing countries than in the industrial countries.[9]

The second reason offered for higher costs—that increasing yields will raise costs because of diminishing returns to fertilizer—is also not a valid one. While higher yields may require more fertilizer per unit of output, it does not follow that real costs will increase because fertilizer is only one of many inputs used in grain production. As yields increase per unit of land, other inputs become more productive and thus contribute to lower costs if the returns to these resources remain constant. In addition, farmers do not continue to operate on a single fertilizer-yield function; the function changes over time. As farmers use fertilizer for longer periods of time, they learn how to use it more effectively through a multitude of adjustments such as better-adapted seed varieties, greater plant density, the timing of applications, the location of fertilizer in the soil, and more effective types of fertilizer.[10]

---

[8] Total cropland (excluding cropland used only for pasture) in the United States in 1950 was 409 million acres; in 1969 total cropland was 384 million acres (H. Thomas Frey, *Major Uses of Land in the United States: Summary for 1969*, USDA Agricultural Economic Report, no. 247, 1973, p. 4). Harvested cropland declined from 352 million acres in 1949 to 286 million acres in 1969 (ibid., p. 9).

[9] Theodore W. Schultz has given strong emphasis to the limited role of land in agricultural production: "only *about one-tenth of the land area of the earth is cropland. If it were still in raw land in its natural state, it would be vastly less productive than it is today.* With incentives to improve this land, the capacity of the land would be increased in most parts of the world much more than it has been to date. In this important sense cropland is not the critical limiting factor in expanding food production.

"The original soils of western Europe, except for the Po valley and some parts of France, were, in general, very poor in quality. They are now highly productive. The original soils of Finland were less productive than most of the nearby parts of the Soviet Union, yet today the croplands of Finland are far superior. The original croplands of Japan were inferior to those of Northern India. Presently, the difference between them is greatly in favor of Japan. There are estimates that the Gangetic Plains of India could, with appropriate investments, produce enough food for a billion people. . . .

"Harsh, raw land is what farmers since time immemorial have started with; what matters most over time, however, are the investments that are made to enhance the productivity of cropland" ("The Food Alternatives before Us: An Economic Perspective" [Agricultural Economics, University of Chicago, paper no. 75:6, May 25, 1974], italics in the original).

[10] In a study of adjustments in the use of nitrogen fertilizer in the corn belt, Wallace Huffman found that a major change in the fertilizer-yield function occurred between 1959 and 1964. The function became much flatter and, even though nitrogen use per acre of corn increased 150 percent between 1959 and 1964, the marginal productivity of nitrogen declined very little. See Huffman,

46

As for the third reason, there is a possibility that the prices of farm inputs having a significant energy component will be substantially higher in the future than in the past. The cost of energy is an important element in fertilizer production cost. Estimates by the Tennessee Valley Authority indicate that a four-fold increase in the price of natural gas—from $0.20 per thousand cubic feet to $1.00 per thousand cubic feet—would increase the plant gate price of a ton of urea by $22 or approximately 24 percent.[11] But there are many other factors that affect the cost of nitrogen fertilizer, including technology, size of plants, and percentage of plant capacity utilized. In fact, with natural gas at $1.00 per thousand cubic feet, the cost of producing nitrogen fertilizer with 1974 technology would be less than producing it with free natural gas and 1960 technology.[12] The TVA estimates indicate that the gate price of urea, with natural gas at $1.00 per thousand cubic feet, for a plant with a capacity of 1,000 tons per day would be less than the price at a plant with a capacity of 600 tons per day with natural gas at $0.40 per thousand cubic feet.[13]

Another factor affecting the cost of fertilizers in the developing countries is the low ratio of output to capacity. In such countries, most of the nitrogen plants operate at between 60 and 70 percent of capacity. If utilization were expanded to the level achieved in the industrial countries—approximately 90 percent—fertilizer costs would decline significantly.[14] This expansion is unlikely, however, if developing countries continue to protect their fertilizer industries, thus imposing unnecessarily high costs on their farmers. Also affecting the output of fertilizers, as will be noted later, is the situation in the

---

"The Contribution of Education and Extension to Differential Rates of Change" (Ph.D. dissertation, Department of Economics, University of Chicago, 1972), pp. 27-34.

[11] Tennessee Valley Authority, "World Fertilizer Market Review and Outlook," in U.S. Senate, Committee on Agriculture and Forestry, *U.S. and World Fertilizer Outlook*, 93rd Cong., 2nd sess., March 21, 1974, p. 106. Natural gas at $0.20/Mcf is equivalent to petroleum at $1.54 per barrel; at $1.00/Mcf the petroleum equivalent is $6.53 per barrel.

[12] For a plant producing 333 tons of urea per day using the older technology, the gate price of a ton of urea, if natural gas were free, would be about $164. With natural gas at $1.00/MCF, the gate price would be $116 for a plant producing 1,667 tons of urea per day. Calculations based on Tennessee Valley Authority, "World Fertilizer Market," p. 104.

[13] Ibid.

[14] According to TVA estimates, the gate price for urea per ton in a plant with 1,667 tons per day capacity operating at 60 percent of capacity is approximately $155 per ton; at 90 percent of capacity, approximately $120 per ton. The calculations assume a price for natural gas of $1.00 per thousand cubic feet. Ibid., pp. 81, 172.

Middle East. Enormous quantities of nitrogen fertilizer could be available at costs comparable to those of recent years if a durable peace were achieved.

Dale Hathaway has made a rather different argument in support of the view that farm prices are likely to be higher in the future than in the past. His argument, at least in part, rests on the political situation that may result from the very substantial increase in farm land prices in the United States since 1970. From early 1972 through early 1974—a period of just two years—the average price of an acre of farm land increased by 42 percent.[15]

It may be very difficult politically to resist measures that would prevent a decline in the absolute level of farm land prices. Hathaway states his position as follows:

> Food prices have contributed heavily to inflation in the past two years; but inflation in turn will maintain or raise food costs for some period ahead. The temporary burst in farm prices to levels above long-run supply prices probably raises the long-run supply price at which equilibrium will finally be reached. The recent inflation will be reflected in higher production costs for farmers, thus introducing a ratchet effect into this cost structure. Moreover, since the higher crop prices are being bid into land prices, there will be irresistible political pressure to maintain farm prices at levels necessary to sustain both asset values and market returns on other resources—even if it means resort to land-retirement programs from time to time over the next few years.[16]

In the first part of the quotation, Hathaway is undoubtedly referring to changes in nominal prices, and such changes need not affect real or deflated prices. The political reaction that he anticipates, however, could affect real prices of farm products for a number of years, at least until the costs of supporting prices above long-run equilibrium levels brought on a reaction similar to that witnessed during the 1960s. At that time, the high cost of the farm commodity programs resulted in substantial modifications of these programs, including a marked reduction in the level of price supports.

The increase in the real price of farm land from 1972 to 1974 was much smaller than the increase in the nominal price. After the

---

[15] U.S. Department of Agriculture, *1974 Handbook of Agricultural Charts*, Agriculture Handbook no. 477, October 1973, p. 13.
[16] Dale E. Hathaway, "Food Prices and Inflation," *Brookings Papers on Economic Activity*, 1974, no. 1, p. 107.

effects of general inflation are taken into account, the increase in the real price, while still substantial, was of the order of 12 percent, or approximately 6 percent annually.[17]

I do not believe that a strong case has been made for expecting significant increases in the real costs of producing grains in the years ahead. The improvements in methods of production that we have seen over the past four decades will continue into the future. There is a major potential for relatively low-cost increases in output in the developing countries if the appropriate conditions are established and if we consider a dynamic rather than a static framework.

Energy Intensity of Agriculture

The agriculture of the industrial countries is often accused of being highly energy intensive and increasingly so over time. In many respects, the technology associated with the use of high-yielding varieties of grain in the developing countries has similar characteristics. Yet, surprisingly, it is not obvious from the data that the agricultural technology associated with the major U.S. grain (corn) was more energy intensive in 1970 than it was a quarter century before. David Pimental and his associates, for example, have estimated that in 1945 the average output of corn in terms of calories was 3.7 per calorie of energy used in producing corn and that by 1970 the ratio had declined to 2.82.[18]

Such a calculation ignores the fact that U.S. corn output was 70 percent greater in 1970 than in 1945. If 1970 corn output had been the same as in 1945, it would have been produced on higher yielding land on the average and, in that case, there would have been energy savings, especially for machinery and gasoline. I do not know if these savings would have offset the actual decline in the ratio of energy output to energy input, but in any event it is not justifiable to compare output to input ratios for such disparate levels of output and to conclude that advances in technology have resulted in a loss of energy productivity. It might also be noted that, although there was no significant change in energy productivity between 1954 and 1970, corn yields nearly doubled. All of the decrease in the ratio

---

[17] The increase in land prices was deflated by the change in the index of family living expenses between the first quarter of 1972 and the first quarter of 1974. U.S. Department of Agriculture, *Agricultural Prices*, February 15 and March 15 issues of 1972 and 1974.

[18] David Pimentel et al., "Food Production and the Energy Crisis," *Science*, vol. 172 (November 2, 1973), p. 445.

of energy output to energy input occurred between 1945 and 1954, when relatively little fertilizer was applied to corn.

To have produced the 1970 corn output with 1945 energy inputs and methods of production would have required almost 140 million acres of corn harvested for grain instead of the 60 million acres actually used in 1970. In effect, a 32 percent increase in energy requirements per bushel of corn "saved" 80 million acres of land. Or to put it another way, if land had been available to produce the 1970 corn output with the 1945 yield, and if all the energy requirements were converted into gallons of gasoline, the use of 1.2 billion gallons of gasoline saved 80 million acres of cropland. Even at 1974 prices, 1.2 billion gallons of gasoline has a value at the refinery of about $325,000,000. Is this an exchange that we would want to make, assuming it were possible? I think not.

Farm Prices Will Decline

I believe the evidence supports the conclusion that farm prices will decline to real levels that are 10 to 20 percent above those prevailing in the early years of the 1970s. In fact, there has already been a substantial decline in the prices of most farm products—wheat, corn, soybeans, cotton, and livestock products. As of early 1975 the prices of grains, livestock products, and cotton have fallen by a third to a half of the peak levels reached in 1973 and 1974.[19] Had it not been for the small feed grain crop in North America in 1974, the decline in grain prices to perhaps half of the peak levels would have occurred before the beginning of 1975.

---

[19] U.S. Department of Agriculture, *Agricultural Prices*, various issues.

6
GRAIN RESERVES AND
PRICE STABILITY

From the end of the Korean War until 1972 the grain reserves of North America served to provide the world's food reserve. These reserves were large enough to give remarkable stability to world grain prices, in the midst of a declining trend in terms of real prices, and were adequate to meet most of the shortfalls in world production that occurred during the two decades. The reserves were not the consequence of deliberate policy decisions by the American and Canadian governments but were the generally unwanted consequences of agricultural price policies. The existence of the reserves in North America made it possible for most of the rest of the world to avoid the cost and bother of holding grain reserves.

Table 10 presents data on wheat, feed grain, and total grain reserves for the major producing areas between 1950 and 1974 and U.S. export prices for wheat and corn for 1955 through 1974. The year-to-year changes in export prices were remarkably small between 1960 and 1971, with the largest percentage annual change being 16 percent for both wheat and corn.

There can be no doubt that substantial reserves of grain can contribute to stability of prices and supplies. In fact, stability of grain prices was achieved over a relatively long period of time and despite rather severe trials. For example, the shortfalls in production below trend that occurred in the world from 1961 through 1965 total more than those that occurred from 1971 through 1974, both in absolute tonnage and in relation to the trend levels of production,[1]

---

[1] From 1961/62 through 1965/66 the net shortfall in world grain production calculated as the algebraic sum of above and below departures from trend was 72 million tons. From 1971/72 through 1974/75 the net shortfall from trend was 36 million tons. Grain production was below trend in 1970/71 because of the corn blight in the United States; if this shortfall is added to the total net shortfall

yet there was relatively little year-to-year variation in the U.S. export prices of grain during the first half of the 1960s (see Table 10). Part of the reason for the greater price stability in the 1960s than in recent years was the significantly larger grain stocks held by the major exporters in 1961 than in 1970 and, especially, in 1972, both absolutely and relatively. In 1961/62 wheat and feed grain stocks held by the major exporters were 14.4 percent of world grain production. In 1970/71 grain stocks were 15.7 percent of world production, and this percentage declined to 10.0 percent in 1972/73. Wheat and feed grain stocks held by the major exporters would have had to equal 170 million tons at the beginning of the 1972/73 crop year to have been as large relative to annual use as such stocks were at the beginning of 1961/62.[2]

Clearly, the major exporters were unwilling to carry such a high level of stocks by themselves. In fact, when wheat and feed grain stocks rose from 70 million tons in 1967 to 105 million tons in 1969, major efforts were made by Australia, Canada, and the United States to reduce the production of wheat.

The annual cost of storing grain, including all costs for putting the grain into storage and taking it out, was approximately $10 per ton as of 1971/72.[3] Of a total grain stock of 170 million tons postulated above, about 30 million tons would constitute an adequate level of working or pipeline stocks for the four major exporters. The cost of storing 140 million tons—the real reserve element out of the total—would thus have been $1.4 billion. As of 1972, neither the private market nor governmental agencies were willing to expend that amount on grain reserves.

Clearly, we can calculate a level of grain reserves that would have prevented most, if not all, of the grain price increases since 1972. At least through the end of 1974, we can say that, if the major exporters had held wheat and feed grain stocks of approximately

for the most recent period, the shortfall was 62 million tons but still less than that for 1961/62 through 1965/66. Calculations were based on data in W. Scott Steele, *The Grain Reserve Issue*, USDA, Foreign Demand and Competition Division Working Paper, July 1974, Tables 3, 4, and 5. Departure from trend for 1974/75 was estimated by the author.

[2] A somewhat different comparison of wheat and feed grain stocks and grain consumption has been made by the Economic Research Service of the U.S. Department of Agriculture. The comparison is between world total wheat and feed grain stocks and world total wheat and feed grain consumption. For 1960/61-1962/63, stocks were 26 percent of consumption; at the beginning of 1972/73, 12 percent. *World Agricultural Situation*, WAS-6, December 1974, p. 29.

[3] Economic Research Service, U.S. Department of Agriculture, *Cost of Storing and Handling Grain and Controlling Dust in Commercial Elevators, 1971/72 . . . Projections for 1973-74*, ERS-513, March 1973, p. 5.

150 million tons and if production levels had been the same in 1972, 1973, and 1974 as they actually were, world and regional grain consumption could have been maintained at trend levels without difficulty. This conclusion assumes that some regions would have increased their grain use above trend level during the period 1972–74.

Why were grain stocks of this size not held? Should not the private market have accumulated much larger reserves than they did? The answer to the second question is an unequivocal no. Governmental interference in grain markets throughout the world during the 1960s and early 1970s, through price supports and control of international trade, has eliminated most of the incentive for private holding of stocks in excess of working stocks from one year to the next. If the changes in year-to-year average prices of wheat and corn in the export markets had been correctly anticipated from 1960 through 1971, there would not have been a single year in which the full costs of storage would have been recovered for either corn or wheat. This does not mean that there would have been no possibility of gain from private storage since annual average prices mask some relevant price variability. But clearly, there would not have been sufficient incentive for private individuals and firms to hold tens of millions of tons of food and feed grains.

In the European Community for the past decade, the private market has had no incentive to hold stocks, except working stocks, because of the limited movement in grain prices from year to year. In effect, whenever governments have a strong influence over the prices of farm products, the private holding of stocks is minimized because of the reduction of potential gain and the increased uncertainty about future prices when they rest on political decisions.

Production Variability and the Need for Reserves

The generally accepted rationale for grain stocks or a world food reserve is similar to that given in 1973 by the director-general of the Food and Agriculture Organization:

> The purpose of the proposal is to ensure that a minimum level of world security is maintained against serious food shortages in periods of crop failure or natural disaster. There are two aspects to this issue. There is the food production problem, which is the concern of a large segment of FAO's regular and field programmes. There is also the separate problem of maintaining a safe level of food stocks to maintain a steady expansion of consumption and to offset

Table 10

WHEAT AND FEED GRAIN STOCKS IN MAJOR EXPORTING COUNTRIES, WORLD GRAIN PRODUCTION, AND U.S. WHEAT AND CORN EXPORT PRICES, 1950–74

Year	Wheat Stocks [a]	Feed Grain Stocks [a]	Total	World Grain Production [b]	U.S. Export Prices ($/metric ton) Wheat	U.S. Export Prices ($/metric ton) Corn [c]
	.... (million tons)			....		
1950–54	30	33	63	[d]	[d]	[d]
1955–59	54	54	108	[d]	62	49
1960	55	73	128	885	62	47
1961	57	82	139	857	60	48
1962	48	69	117	906	64	53
1963	47	63	110	902	65	55
1964	40	69	109	949	65	56
1965	40	54	94	946	59	56
1966	27	43	70	1,013	67	57
1967	31	39	70	1,053	63	48
1968	36	48	84	1,096	63	51
1969	53	52	105	1,099	53	56

1970	60	52	112	1,115	61	61
1971	45	38	83	1,109	60	53
1972	41	52	93	1,083	86	85
1973	23	37	60	1,181	178	118
1974	19	28	47	1,123 [e]	—	—

[a] Stocks at beginning of crop year for Australia, Canada, Argentina, and the United States.
[b] Includes rice in milled form; stock estimates do not include rice.
[c] Crop years—July to June for wheat; October to September for corn.
[d] Data not available on comparable basis.
[e] Preliminary estimate.

Sources: *World Agricultural Situation*, Supplement, October 1972, p. 8 (U.S. corn stocks adjusted from July 1 to October 1); *World Agricultural Situation*, WAS-6, December 1974, pp. 28, 29; *Wheat Situation*, various issues; USDA Statistical Bulletin, no. 423, April 1968, pp. 28–29 (food grain statistics through 1967); *Feed Situation*, November 1974, p. 38. All publications are issued by the Economic Research Service of the U.S. Department of Agriculture.

the year-to-year fluctuations in output which occur and which will continue to occur even when the world production problem is solved. It is this latter aspect—minimum food stocks—on which the present proposal is centered.[4]

Grain and food reserves, according to the director-general, are needed because of year-to-year fluctuations in food production. This might explain why an individual nation might have a food reserve, but it is not an adequate reason for significant reserves for the world. Year-to-year fluctuations in world grain production are relatively small and would not, if there were free trade in grains, make the holding of grain reserves in excess of working stocks an economic investment more than one year out of five.

Research on optimal grain reserves conducted by Yagil Danin, Daniel Sumner, and myself indicates that year-to-year variations in world grain production would result in a need for world grain reserves in, at most, one year out of five, and in only one year out of twenty would such reserves exceed 10 million tons.[5] We assumed that reserves were optimal when the expected gain equalled the expected cost of holding an additional ton of grain. Our analysis did not include the effects of demand variability, nor did it take into account the effects of destruction of crop output by floods, storms, or other natural disasters. But demand variations are small, especially for the food grains, and the amount of reserves required for post-harvest disasters would be modest.

The basic reason why world grain or food reserves are required is, therefore, not fluctuation in production. It is, instead, the governmental policies that prevent ready access to the available supplies of grain. Potential purchasers are prevented access by export controls, which exist in almost all countries. Governments may also interfere by entering the world market to purchase grain at one price and then reselling it into the domestic market at a lower price, as has been the practice in recent years in the European Community, the Soviet Union, and China. In other words, the price system has not been permitted to operate to allocate grain, and this is the primary reason for the need to hold reserves. While there is relatively little possibility that governmental policies affecting grain prices and supplies will change in the near future, it at least seems desirable to recognize

---

[4] Director-General, Food and Agriculture Organization, *World Food Security: Proposal of the Director-General*, C 7.3/17, August 1973, p. 3.

[5] Yagil Danin, Daniel Sumner and D. Gale Johnson, "Determination of Optimal Grain Carryovers" (Office of Agricultural Economic Research, University of Chicago, paper no. 74:12, revised, March 25, 1975), p. 27.

the primary reason why most reserves that have been and will be held have had a useful function.

Possible Roles for Grain Reserves

If we assume that governmental interferences with trade in farm products will be eliminated slowly, if at all, there are both economic and humanitarian reasons for holding grain reserves, by individual countries, by an international agency, or by agreement among a number of individual countries. Without attempting to develop the ideas in any depth, I believe that there are three important roles for grain reserves.

Emergency Reserves for the Developing Countries. For a variety of reasons, developing countries may not hold sufficient reserves for achieving the desired stability of supplies. The reasons may involve financial or bureaucratic failure or price policies that prevent the private market from carrying the optimal level of reserves. Or the government may decide to vary imports or exports to offset variations in domestic production only to find that external interferences with grain prices and trade have made the available foreign exchange inadequate for the desired imports. If grain prices had remained at 50 percent of their 1971/72 level through 1974, for example, the developing countries with production shortfalls during that period would have had little difficulty, with the possible exception of Bangladesh, in importing enough grain to prevent hardship.

One proposal worthy of consideration is that high-income countries assure each developing country or region that they will make up all grain production shortfalls in a given year in excess of a given percentage of trend production. Somewhat arbitrarily, the figure incorporated in the proposal was a shortfall in excess of 6 percent of trend production. This proposal, which might be called an international insurance reserve, would not eliminate the desirability of reserves in individual developing countries but would reduce the optimal reserve levels quite significantly.

In an example worked out for India for the period from 1948 through 1973, it was found that total grain payments of 13 million tons would have reduced the maximum optimal carryover levels from 12 million tons to 6 million tons and would have prevented any shortfall in annual consumption below trend level in excess of 5 million tons, or about 7 percent. In only three years would there have been shortfalls of between 3 and 5 million tons. Over the twenty-six-year period, additional total grain imports of 3 million tons would have held consumption shortfalls to a maximum of 3 million tons.[6]

It might be desirable to have an additional small reserve, held partly as financial resources and partly as physical commodities, to meet emergencies that arise out of other variations in crop supplies. Natural disasters, such as floods, hurricanes, and earthquakes, require the rapid availability of food if human suffering is to be minimized. Generally, the major difficulties in such situations are problems of transportation and local distribution and not the availability of supplies. The proper positioning of supplies could aid in reducing the lag between an emergency and the relief effort.

Grain Reserves and Freer Trade. The major grain exporters, including the United States, may find it profitable to establish reserves as part of a bargaining process for the reduction of barriers to trade in farm products. At best, it is going to be difficult to induce the major importers of Western Europe and Japan to reduce their barriers to trade and increase their dependence upon other areas of the world for an increasing fraction of their food supply. To have any significant chance of achieving such reductions, the major exporters must be able to convince the major importers that the former will be reliable suppliers at reasonable and relatively stable prices.[7]

Commercial Contingencies. The size of the reserves required to absorb variations in import demand from the generally permanent grain importers—Western Europe, Japan, and countries around the edge of Asia (for example, Taiwan, Malaysia)—would be relatively modest. An analysis has not yet been made to indicate the size of the reserve required for this purpose.

It is highly probable that, if the Soviet Union either were excluded from the world grain markets or operated its own optimal grain reserve program, the reserves adequate to hold variations in world grain trade within narrow limits would be quite small—perhaps no more than 10 to 15 million tons. This conclusion is based on the assumption that reserves earmarked for assistance to developing countries would be held separately. But the Soviet Union will not be excluded from world grain markets, and if the Soviet Union does not operate its own grain reserve program, world grain markets will be

---

[6] Ibid., pp. 21-24.

[7] The argument for such a reserve has been made in *Toward the Integration of World Agriculture*, A Tripartite Report by Fourteen Experts from North America, the European Community, and Japan (Washington, D.C.: Brookings Institution, October 1973), pp. 23-27. I was one of the fourteen "experts."

subjected to significant shocks and—based on the past distributions of Soviet grain production—probably somewhat more often than once a decade. Thus, it may be in the interest of consumers to hold a grain reserve to protest against large-scale Soviet grain imports. Such an additional reserve might amount to 20 million tons today and it would grow over time as Soviet grain output increased.

Rebuilding Reserves

When should grain reserves be rebuilt? One response has been that efforts should have already been made.[8] I believe that food reserves, especially reserves to meet the emergency needs of the developing countries, should be accumulated only when supplies have become more plentiful and prices significantly lower than they were in 1974 and early 1975.

If an effort had been made to build reserves in 1974, for example, grain prices would have significantly increased. This effect would have placed additional burdens on those developing countries that found it necessary to import grain in 1973/74 and 1974/75. Given the sensitivity of grain markets to relatively small pieces of bad news during most of 1974, an announcement that the United States was going to set aside as a reserve 5 million tons of grain could easily have increased grain prices by 10 percent.

World grain reserves have been and are at critically low levels, so low that a below-normal world grain crop in 1974 resulted in substantial price increases. Until reserves are rebuilt, this precarious situation will continue. But before reserves are rebuilt by governmental actions, we must wait for a significant decline in grain prices. Only then can a reserve program be instituted that will not do great harm to those whom it is supposed to benefit.

---

[8] Lester R. Brown recommended that "the [U.S.] Department of Agriculture might start building up at least a minimal level of reserve stocks to provide a margin of safety next year, even though prices are high" (U.S. Senate, Committee on Agriculture and Forestry, Subcommittees on Agricultural Production, Marketing, and Stabilization of Prices and on Foreign Agricultural Policy, *Hearings on U.S. and World Food Situation*, 93rd Cong., 1st sess., October 1973, p. 103).

7

INCREASING FOOD PRODUCTION IN THE DEVELOPING COUNTRIES

There is a large potential for expanding food production in the developing countries. In the materials prepared for the World Food Conference, one finds the following:

> The only viable strategy for effectively tackling the food problems in the future is, therefore, to put the maximum possible priority on objectives, policies and programmes for increasing food production within the developing countries, and to achieve rates of growth substantially above recent trends. This strategy is not just based on hopes and expectations, but it is supported by an analysis of the potentials for food production waiting exploitation in the developing countries.[1]

The important issue here is not whether the developing countries can maintain a rate of growth in food output approximately equal to the rate of population growth. This goal would be achievable on the basis of continuation of existing policies and recent trends in production, and the recent trends in production can be assumed to continue for the next decade or so, with a high degree of probability. The issue is, instead, whether the world has the capacity to do better than maintain the status quo and to achieve a significant improvement in per capita food supply for poorer people by the end of this century. How large the increase in per capita food supply might be depends not only upon growth in food output but also upon the rate of population growth. In my opinion, the conclusion that the improvement in per capita food supply by the end of this century will be modest

---

[1] World Food Conference, United Nations, *The World Food Problem: Proposals for National and International Action*, E/CONF. 65/4, 1974, pp. 23-24; hereinafter referred to as World Food Conference, *Proposals*.

unless there is some reduction in the rate of population growth in the developing countries is inescapable.

It is instructive to compare the development of yields in the industrial and developing countries over the past four decades. During the years 1934–38 grain yields per hectare were the same in both sets of countries, approximately 1.15 tons. Between 1934–38 and 1952-56, grain yields were static in the developing countries, but increased in the industrial countries to 1.37 metric tons per hectare. During 1969/70, grain yields in the industrial countries averaged 2.14 tons and in the developing countries, 1.41 tons. It is worth noting that grain yields in the developing countries in 1969/70 were slightly higher than in the industrial countries in 1952–56.[2]

The much higher grain yields in the industrial countries as of the 1970s do not appear to be due to more favorable weather or soil. In fact, the developing countries have a much greater opportunity for double and triple cropping in the same year than the temperate-zone industrial countries, and thus their potential annual production from a hectare of cultivated land is almost certainly greater.

I am cautiously optimistic that the per capita food supplies of the world's poorer people can be improved. But, as I shall argue in the last chapter, there must be the necessary political will in both the industrial and the developing countries if this potential is to be realized. The problems of achieving an improved world food situation must be taken seriously, and they must be considered as long-run problems that can be solved only by continuous attention.

What Have We Learned?

A great deal can be learned from the efforts of the past few years to improve the food production capabilities of the developing countries. The lessons are there if we only have the wisdom to find them.

The first lesson is that, if certain efforts are made, agricultural research can have a high payoff for the developing countries, just as it did for the industrial countries. It should be noted that the increase in yields of grain crops in the industrial countries is a relatively recent phenomenon. The yields of two major grains in the United States— corn and wheat—were the same during the 1920s as during the 1870s. Grain yields in England in the early part of the twentieth

---

[2] Grain yields were estimated from data in Food and Agriculture Organization, *Production Yearbook*, various issues. China is included.

century were no greater than in the mid-nineteenth century. Only Japan achieved significant yield increases in the nineteenth century.[3]

While there has been some form of agricultural research for centuries, publicly supported research is little more than a century old, and it was not until well into the third decade of this century that public expenditures for agricultural research in the United States reached $25 million.[4] Hybrid corn, the first major high-yielding grain variety, became commercially available only four decades ago. Hybrid sorghum, the second of the major high-yielding grains, has been available for less than two decades. Until fairly recently, almost all investment in agricultural research was made in North America, Japan, and Northern Europe. Significant investment in agricultural research in the developing countries began to occur only after World War II and only in a few countries. The highly successful cooperative effort between the Rockefeller Foundation and the Mexican government was started in 1943. It was out of this program that the dwarf wheats emerged in 1963. Dwarf wheats are now seeded on about a third of the total wheat area in nine developing countries and are responsible for at least half of the total wheat output in those countries. Included in the nine countries are India, Pakistan, Turkey, and Mexico.

While some scientific achievements do have universal relevance for agriculture, much additional research is generally required to solve problems that are specific to a particular location. Thus, while hybridization has universal application and significance, the best results can be obtained only when plants have been developed for rather restricted geographic areas. Differences in rainfall, altitude, length of day, length of growing season, and temperature ranges and variations are important—apparently far, far more important to the optimum development of plants than to man. A significant research effort is required in virtually all agricultural areas to find and maintain plant varieties that resist locally prevalent diseases and insects. One of the major risks that was accepted in the rapid adoption of the

---

[3] Lester R. Brown, *Increasing World Food Output: Problems and Prospects,* USDA Foreign Agricultural Economic Report, no. 25, April 1965, pp. 13-21. While at several points throughout this monograph, I have been critical of positions taken by Mr. Brown, I want to say that I have learned a great deal from the publication cited above and his *Man, Land & Food,* USDA Foreign Agricultural Economic Report, no. 11, November 1963. It can be said that, had the advice and constructive suggestions made by Brown in these two publications been followed, I would not now be writing these words.

[4] Robert Evenson, "The Contribution of Agricultural Research and Extension to Agricultural Production" (Ph.D. dissertation, Department of Economics, University of Chicago, 1968), p. 3.

new high-yielding varieties of rice and wheat was that these varieties, while relatively resistant to the major diseases and insects of the area where they had been developed, might be susceptible to heavy losses in the areas to which they were transplanted. Fortunately for millions of people, catastrophe did not occur.

Most of the world's publicly supported agricultural research is still undertaken in the industrial countries and not in the developing countries. According to estimates made by Robert Evenson and Yoav Kislev, only 15 percent of the world's public expenditures on agricultural research in 1970 was spent in Africa, Latin America and Asia (China excluded).[5] These areas have 75 percent of the world's population and an even higher fraction of the world's farm population (China excluded). The enormous disparity in annual research investment is indicated by a comparison of public research expenditures per farm in 1965: $93 in North America, $32 in Northern Europe, $0.43 in South Asia, and $1.50 in South America.[6] The cost of research is somewhat smaller in the developing countries than in the industrial countries, but if research input is measured in scientific man-years instead of dollars, the discrepancy on a per farm basis between North America and South Asia narrows only slightly to 72 to 1.

If the developing countries are to approach the grain yield levels of the industrial countries, the agricultural research effort in these countries must increase many times above the present level. More research effort is not all that is required, but such a quantitative approach seems to be a necessary condition for successful and relatively low-cost expansion of the food supply.

A second lesson that we have learned in the past few years, though the evidence was there long before, is that poor farmers, even those tens of millions who are either illiterate or barely literate, do indeed respond to new and profitable opportunities and can quickly adopt highly complicated production technologies with which they have had no prior experience. Such farmers have disproved—hopefully once and for all—the derogatory and negative stereotypes held by many planners, governmental officials, and others whom I have on occasion referred to as urban intellectuals.

We may also have learned a third lesson—that there is no such thing as a free lunch or a really low-cost lunch when it comes to

[5] Robert E. Evenson and Yoav Kislev, *Agricultural Research and Productivity* (New Haven, Conn.: Yale University Press, forthcoming), Chap. 2. Data on number of farms are from FAO, *Production Yearbook, 1971*, pp. 10-11.
[6] Ibid.

increasing food production. Research developments almost never stand by themselves. If we tried to grow the existing hybrid varieties of corn that now yield at least 100 bushels per acre (6 tons per hectare) throughout most of the American corn belt with the same complementary inputs used forty years ago, yields would be little higher than then—about 40 bushels per acre (2.5 tons per hectare). Much research, especially that dealing with plant varieties, acts primarily to increase potential yield; this potential can be realized only as other inputs are made available. Thus, the process of achieving higher yields per unit of land and greater total food output in the developing countries depends on many things besides more research, essential as research is.

A fourth lesson we must learn is that governments do have the capacity to react to new opportunities that can lead to an improvement in their food situation. Admittedly, their responses have not been as rapid or as purposeful as those of farmers. But throughout the developing countries, numerous examples exist of governments that have made available, either by local production or importation, the essential complementary inputs of fertilizer, insecticides, electricity, diesel fuel, pumps, and pipe for tube wells. I am not suggesting that in all countries policy accommodations have been made. Some governments still interfere with prices and with incentives to increase production in an effort to maintain a cheap food policy. But even when they do, their recent actions have been less adverse to food production than those engaged in a decade ago.

A fifth lesson that I hope we have learned is that large-scale food aid, such as the Public Law 480 program during the latter half of the 1950s and the first half of the 1960s contributes very little to the food supply of the developing countries. The lower prices that result from food aid have some disincentive effects for farmers in the developing countries, but perhaps more important is the effect of such food aid on governments, which may continue to follow policies that are adverse to the increase of domestic production. We must support food aid to meet emergencies resulting from adverse weather or other natural disasters, but we should also realize that food aid in normal times has few real long-term benefits for the recipient countries.

Steps to Increase Food Production

There are several important measures that can be taken to increase food production in the developing countries and to achieve a rate of growth of production in excess of the population growth rate. Space permits only very brief consideration of each.[7]

Agricultural Research. Agricultural research has had a major role in more than doubling grain yields in the industrial countries over the past four decades. Obviously, many other factors have had their role—the reduction in fertilizer costs, improved pest and disease controls, and more effective control of weeds. But for all of these factors, the research results can be said to have been a necessary condition. Without hybrid corn, for example, lower-cost fertilizer would have had only a modest impact on yields.

If we and the other industrial nations are willing to assist in increasing the food supply in the developing countries, we should support a major expansion in agricultural research in the developing areas. Research must occur in the developing countries, as we have noted before, because agriculture is location-specific. In most instances, plant varieties cannot be easily transferred from one climatic zone to another. Each climatic and soil area has specific problems that must be solved if agricultural resources are to be utilized effectively. It is the exception when a plant variety that gives high yields in Iowa will even survive in India.

Consequently, the developing countries need the capacity to undertake their own research, both basic and applied. Basic research is required since it contributes to the quality of applied research, both directly and through the education of scientists.

The necessary expenditures are not large. It has been estimated that total world expenditures for publicly supported agricultural research in 1965 were less than a billion dollars; private research relevant to agriculture almost certainly amounted to less than that. What is required is a long-term commitment by the United States and other industrial countries to provide support for agricultural research throughout Africa, Latin America, and Asia. At the present time, the United States does not seem to have the capacity to provide foreign aid on an annual basis, let alone make a commitment for a decade. Our government wants quick results, and as a consequence we are always disappointed.

There are a number of multilateral and bilateral ways in which the industrial countries could assist agricultural research. One such way is through regional centers, and in fact, a great part of international funding of agricultural research, both private and public, is

---

[7] For more complete discussion of these and other measures, I refer the interested reader to World Food Conference, *Proposals.*

already going to such centers. While regional centers are important and can make significant contributions, it would help greatly if national research capabilities were developed. Only such capabilities can develop varieties that fit local conditions, continue to fight the area's specific insects and diseases, encourage independent discovery, and create centers for developing the scientists and researchers of the future.

There are a number of particular research programs that deserve the highest priority. Root crops, which serve as the main food for about a tenth of the world's population, have received little emphasis. As will be noted later, a major research effort is required to eliminate the tsetse fly from middle Africa. We know relatively little about the production of food crops in tropical areas. The challenges are many; the opportunities are enormous.

There are substantial risks involved when new grain varieties are introduced into agricultural regions that lack viable agricultural research institutions. These institutions are needed to modify the varieties as they become susceptible to local disease and insects, as they inevitably will. These institutions are also needed to develop varieties to meet local tastes—as, for example, in South Asia where it has been necessary to modify the high-yielding varieties of rice to suit particular taste patterns. When one grain is the major food, it should be a grain that is liked. It is important to keep in mind that even very poor people have their likes and dislikes.

If the industrial nations were to commit themselves to provide $1 billion annually for a decade and one-half of that amount for the subsequent decade, great strides could be made to bring the benefits of agricultural research to all the major climatic zones of the developing world. Additional scientists would have to be trained first, but anyone who is familiar with academic life in the United States knows that the facilities for such training are readily available.

Supply of Modern Farm Inputs. The fact that the industrial countries have substantially higher yields of grain than the developing countries is not due to the greater intelligence of our farmers, to the better quality of our land, or to a more satisfactory climate. The higher yields can be explained primarily by the availability of modern farm inputs such as fertilizer, advanced seed varieties adapted to climatic and soil conditions, pesticides, herbicides, more adequate water control where irrigation is used, and to a much smaller degree, the replacement of animal and human power by mechanical power.

The availability of modern farm inputs is dependent on agricultural research, but not solely. Governments must provide a political and economic setting in which such inputs are available if there is a demand for them and at prices that are related to the costs of obtaining such inputs through international trade. All too many of the developing countries protect industries that produce fertilizer or farm machines and, as a result, impose high costs upon farmers and consumers.

It is often argued that, because of the current world energy situation, it would be a mistake to transfer the energy-intensive agricultural technology of North America or Western Europe to the developing countries. But at least for the next two decades, according to the knowledge we have now, there is no other way to achieve substantial increases in food production in the developing countries. There must be large increases in fertilizer use—at least a doubling of use in the developing countries in the next decade. Energy will have to be used to increase irrigation water and to obtain better control of existing water. It is unlikely that in most of the developing countries tractors will replace a significant fraction of animal and human power within the next two decades, but the amount of energy required would not be very great even if the replacement were made. Available data indicate that more energy is used to produce fertilizer in the United States than is required for the operation of all the tractors and trucks on farms.

And if energy saving is required, there are almost certainly ways to achieve it while providing sufficient supplies to agriculture. It has been estimated that in the United States more energy is consumed in shopping for food than is used on farms in producing the food!

Fertilizer Supply. The crucial role of fertilizer in the increased production of food in the developing countries needs further discussion. An important recent concern, growing out of the higher prices of energy and the possibilities of exhausting the available supplies, has been the fear that it will not be possible to realize the necessary expansion of fertilizer output. Each of the main fertilizer nutrients— nitrogen, phosphates, and potash—require substantial amounts of energy for their production and processing. In fact, for the production of nitrogen, almost the only input is energy, most often in the form of natural gas. While the raw materials for phosphate and potash are the result of mining operations, the processing of both, and especially phosphate, requires significant energy inputs.[8]

In order to increase food production in the developing countries to a level slightly higher than population growth between 1970 and 1985 (2.6 percent versus 2.4 percent), it has been estimated that fertilizer consumption in those countries will have to more than double during the 1970s.[9] And the industrial countries will be increasing their fertilizer use as well, by perhaps 50 to 60 percent.

In the materials presented to the World Food Conference in 1974, it was estimated that there would be substantial shortfalls in fertilizer supplies by 1980/81. The amounts of the shortfalls were based on estimates prepared by the World Bank Group from data available as of September 1973. The indicated shortfalls (in terms of plant nutrients) were 18.8 million tons of nitrogen and 10.4 million tons of phosphates. In each case, the shortfall was approximately a third of projected requirements.[10]

But changes in the capacity to produce nitrogen fertilizer have been occurring with remarkable speed. Estimates made by the Tennessee Valley Authority indicate that, between December 1973 and April 1974, the effective capacity of nitrogen plants as of 1980 had been increased from 56.3 million tons to 66.9 million tons. Between April and August 1974, "perhaps an additional 6.4 million tons has been contracted or planned." [11] Included in the estimates of additional capacity after April 1974 were eight large ammonia plants that the U.S.S.R. contracted with Western engineering firms. In July 1974 Saudi Arabia announced plans for new nitrogen plants totaling about 1 million tons of capacity by 1980.[12] The firm additions to the 1980 nitrogen supply that have been made since late 1973 total about

---

[8] In the unpublished paper written by Pimentel and associates, which served as the basis of Pimentel et al., "Food Production and the Energy Crisis," *Science*, vol. 172 (November 2, 1973), estimates were given of the total energy requirements for a pound of plant nutrients, including production, processing, and mining, where relevant. In terms of kilocalories, the energy requirements per pound were as follows: nitrogen, 8,400; phosphorous, 1,520; and potassium, 1,050. A gallon of gasoline, which weighs approximately eight pounds, has 36,225 kilocalories.

[9] World Food Conference, *Proposals*, pp. 38-39.

[10] Ibid.

[11] Economic Research Service, U.S. Department of Agriculture, *The World Fertilizer Situation: 1975, 1976 and 1980*, Supplement to *World Agricultural Situation*, WAS-5, September 1974, p. 13.

[12] Economic Research Service, *World Fertilizer Situation*, p. 13. The measure of increase in capacity is for effective capacity, assuming achievable rates of capacity utilization and deductions of 20 percent for industrial use in the industrial countries and 10 percent in the developing countries.

18 million tons, or approximately the shortfall projected by the World Bank Group for 1980/81. The magnitude of the planned or contracted expansion of nitrogen fertilizer production is clear when it is remembered that total nitrogen production in 1970 was 30 million tons.

The past growth rates in the use of phosphate and potash fertilizers have been significantly smaller than that of nitrogen, and this relation is expected to continue into the future. The production of phosphate and potash requires mining of specific raw materials, but in both cases available supplies seem adequate for the foreseeable future. As with nitrogen, the World Bank Group foresaw a significant shortfall in phosphate supplies as of 1980/81; no projections were made for potash. The U.S. Department of Agriculture projections for both phosphate and potash indicate adequate supplies by 1980, though the margin of adequacy is small.[13]

Peace in the Middle East and fertilizer production and prices. While I argued in Chapter 5 that the impact of higher energy prices on the costs of producing nitrogen fertilizer has probably been greatly exaggerated, for the longer run it makes an important difference whether the plant gate price of urea is $90 or $120 per ton. A stable and durable peace in the Middle East could contribute in a major way to the availability of nitrogen fertilizer—the plant nutrient with the fastest growing demand. The lowest cost area for producing nitrogen fertilizer in the world is in the Middle East—or at least that is potentially so. The Middle East has enormous reserves of natural gas that could serve as the energy input for a large fraction of the world's output of nitrogen fertilizer. More natural gas is flared (wasted) in the Middle East than is consumed by the entire petrochemical industry in the United States. Nitrogen fertilizer is part of the output of the U.S. petrochemical industry, and we now produce about a quarter of the world's supply.

It has been estimated that the amount of natural gas flared by the members of the Organization of Petroleum Exporting Countries (OPEC)—and thus primarily in the Middle East—would supply the energy input for more than 110 million tons of nitrogen in fertilizers.[14] The world's consumption of nitrogen in fertilizers in 1970/71 was 33 million tons, and the projected consumption for 1980 is approximately 60 million tons.[15]

---

[13] Ibid., pp. 21-30.
[14] World Food Conference, *Proposals*, pp. 39, 45.
[15] Ibid., p. 39.

While nitrogen fertilizer production has been increased in the Middle East over the past decade—and while further expansion is planned—the unstable political and military situation has been a barrier to making the required large capital investments.[16] But given a durable peace, there is no reason why such investments would not be made and a very large supply of relatively low-cost nitrogen fertilizer made available. Obviously, it is not essential that all or even most of the natural gas that is now being wasted in the Middle East be used for the production of nitrogen. If only a fifth of it were so used, the effect on the supplies of nitrogen fertilizer and prices would be evident for more than the next decade.

Fertilizer prices in 1973 and 1974. While it is somewhat of a digression, it may be useful to say a few words about fertilizer price increases after 1972. Some may feel that an optimistic view of future fertilizer supplies is inconsistent with the two- and three-fold increases in prices since 1972.[17] The increase in fertilizer prices has been the result of two factors—the sharp increase in grain and other crop prices and the very low short-run elasticity of fertilizer supply. However, the increased cost of energy has been responsible for no more than a tenth of the increase in the price of fertilizer. An expansion of fertilizer production requires a significant lead time, and fertilizer producers were no more omniscient about the grain and food prices of 1973 and 1974 than the rest of us.

The following rather long quotation from a recent review of the world fertilizer situation by the Tennessee Valley Authority is both interesting and convincing:

> The world fertilizer market was relatively stable during the 1960–65 period. However, drought caused food shortages in certain areas and was interpreted by some to be the beginning of a world food crisis. In addition new fertilizer pro-

---

[16] The Tennessee Valley Authority has estimated that the plant investment for the production of 550,000 tons of urea per year, for a plant started in 1974 and completed in 1977, in a developing country was $104 million if the feedstock for ammonia production was natural gas. Since the nitrogen content of urea is 46 percent, the capital investment per million tons of nitrogen is estimated at slightly more than $200 million. In this example, it was assumed that the plant operated at 90 percent of capacity. See Tennessee Valley Authority, "World Fertilizer Market Review and Outlook," in U.S. Senate, Committee on Agriculture and Forestry, *U.S. and World Fertilizer Outlook*, 93rd Cong., 2nd sess., March 21, 1974, p. 104, for the estimate of plant investment.

[17] In 1970 the Agency for International Development paid about $75 per ton for bagged urea; in 1974 it paid from $300 to $375 per ton. The price increase for phosphate fertilizers was even greater, from about $50 per ton to $300 to $375 per ton. Economic Research Service, *World Fertilizer Situation*, p. 9. Figures were interpolated from a graph.

ducing technology had been developed and idle capital was quickly pumped into what looked like an opportunity for sustained large-scale returns. Many production units were built, first in the developed regions and later in many of the developing countries. The result was an oversupply of fertilizers—with low prices, distress selling, and poor returns on investment. This lasted into the 1970's when demand again caught up with supplies.

These profitless years led to caution throughout the industry; lack of new investment; closing of old, inefficient plants; and delays or abandonment of new projects. As a result, when demand surged in 1972 and 1973, there was no additional capacity readily available to supply the market. Nations that traditionally had sold internationally reduced export shipments to meet the domestic demand; importing countries, accustomed to a buyer's market, found that they could not go out on the spur of the moment and obtain whatever quantity or type of material they wanted. Currently, the world fertilizer market is a seller's market; however, past performance suggests that these situations do not last long and that changes can be expected.[18]

Expansion of the Cultivated Area. The emphasis of this analysis has been on what is required to expand output per unit of land and, indirectly, per unit of all resources engaged in food production. Until World War II, most of the increase in the world's food output resulted from increases in cultivated area. Even since World War II, expansion of the cultivated area has been approximately as important as increased yields in boosting food production in the developing countries.[19] Starting in the early 1960s, however, increases in grain yields dominated output growth in the developing countries, as it had for some time in the industrial countries.[20]

As was noted in Chapter 5, it is quite possible that in the future most of the developing countries will find it less costly to expand food and grain output by achieving higher yields than by expanding

---

[18] Tennessee Valley Authority, "World Fertilizer Market Review," p. 68.

[19] The Economic Research Service of the U.S. Department of Agriculture estimated that in the developing countries (excluding China) grain production increased 78 percent between 1948-52 and 1966-70. For the same period of time, grain yields increased 32 percent and grain area, 35 percent (*World Food Situation and Prospects to 1985*, Foreign Agricultural Economic Report, no. 98, December 1974, p. 65).

[20] From data supplied by the Economic Research Service on grain area, yields, and production in the developing countries (excluding China) in 1960-62 and 1969-71, I estimated that grain area increased by 13 percent and yield by 20 percent, resulting in a 36 percent increase in production.

the cultivated area. Yet the potential for expanding the cultivated area in the developing countries is worth considering. In 1969 the Food and Agriculture Organization completed a major study of the possibilities for expanding food production in the developing countries. As a part of that study, a careful analysis was made of the potential cultivatable area of the developing countries. The FAO concluded that there are 1,145 million hectares of land suitable for crops, more than twice the 512 million hectares devoted to crops in 1962. While most of this potential is in Africa and Latin America, it was estimated that countries in Asia and the Far East could also increase their cultivated area by approximately a sixth.[21]

Materials prepared for the World Food Conference indicate that a reasonable target for expansion of the cultivated area in the developing countries is an increase by 1985 of 140 million hectares over the 737 million hectares cultivated in 1970.[22] The land that could be added is not equally divided among the developing regions. The most promising and largest areas are the Amazon basin, the Mekong basin, southern Sudan, and the area affected by the tsetse fly in middle Africa.[23] Most of the new land development over the next decade, however, is likely to occur in areas other than these, although by the end of this century some of these areas may also be added. But one must note that there are many problems to be solved and large investments that must be made before the potential doubling of crop area can be realized.

A brief description of production potentials in the area in middle Africa affected by the tsetse fly may be of interest. It is estimated that 7 million square kilometers (1.7 billion acres) of agricultural land could be added to the world's supply. This is an enormous area, actually larger than the total agricultural area of the United States.[24]

The tsetse fly causes trypanosomiasis (sleeping sickness) in both livestock and humans. In most countries of the world, sleeping sickness has been brought under control, but the problem is of such enormous proportions in middle Africa that even a large-scale program of research and implementation might take two decades to conquer it. The most promising avenue currently available is chem-

---

[21] Food and Agriculture Organization, *Provisional Indicative World Plan for Agricultural Development* (Rome, 1969), vol. 1, p. 49. China was not included in estimates of either the potential or actual cultivated area.

[22] World Food Conference, *Proposals*, p. 64. China was included in the data.

[23] Ibid., pp. 64-65.

[24] Ibid., pp. 72-75. In 1969 the total land in farms in the United States was 1.06 billion acres; in addition, there were 287 million acres of grazing land not in farms. U.S. Department of Agriculture, *Agricultural Statistics*, 1973, p. 425.

ical control, although biological methods of eliminating the tsetse fly might cost less in the long run. If the tsetse fly were eliminated, the first use of the area would probably be for increasing beef production, but over time, much of the land could be devoted to crops. It has been estimated that the cattle population could be increased by 120 million head—approximately the number of cattle in the United States in 1973—although meat production would reach only 1.5 million tons annually.[25]

Irrigation—Improvements and Expansion. Currently, there are about 93 million hectares of land in the developing countries that receive some form of irrigation. Studies have concluded, however, that "a large number of irrigation schemes are operating at less than 50 percent efficiency and the doubling of staple food crop yields, such as cereals, with improved management of the necessary inputs is perfectly feasible in many areas."[26]

The improvement and expansion of irrigation requires substantial capital investments. Renovating 46 million hectares of existing irrigated area has been estimated to cost $21 billion; irrigating an additional 23 million hectares would cost $38 billion.[27] In these calculations it was assumed that the renovation and new construction of a total of 69 million hectares could be accomplished by 1985.

The new high-yielding varieties of crops have been most productive on irrigated land, and for optimum yields, effective water control is required. One of the characteristics of the high-yielding varieties of rice and wheat is short height. Wide variations in the depth of water either make the use of these varieties impossible or subject them to the risk of being destroyed by high water. Thus, in many countries, further expansion of the high-yielding varieties requires improvements in irrigation systems.

Adequate Incentives for Farmers. The growth of food production will be disappointing unless farmers are provided with adequate incentives. The ready availability of the products of agricultural

---

[25] Beef production in the United States has been approximately 10 million tons, carcass weight, in recent years. For the estimate of beef production after eliminating the tsetse fly, see World Food Conference, *Proposals*, p. 72; for U.S. beef production, see U.S. Department of Agriculture, *Agricultural Statistics, 1973*, p. 349.

[26] World Food Conference, *Proposals*, p. 62.

[27] Ibid., p. 67.

research, renovated and expanded irrigation, and a ready supply of modern farm inputs is not enough. The utilization of these services and products must be profitable. These must seem like self-evident statements, and they are.

It may be argued that the term "adequate incentives" is so imprecise as to be meaningless. Actually, it is not difficult to determine whether a government is following short-run and shortsighted policies of holding down the prices of major farm products and pushing up the prices of modern farm inputs. India, for example, has generally held the farm price of rice below world prices and that of wheat above world prices. It is not surprising, therefore, that the new high-yielding varieties of rice have not been adopted as rapidly or as extensively as the new wheats. What is surprising is that there has been so little analysis of these policies that exploit farmers and so little criticism of governments that put them into practice.

International Trade Liberalization. It is only infrequently that a link is made between the liberalization of international trade and per capita food supplies in the developing countries. It is unfortunate that there is so little understanding of the role of trade in increasing incomes and food supplies in the developing countries. The industrial countries have been willing to go a considerable distance in removing barriers to trade among themselves in industrial products, but they have been most reluctant to lower the barriers to imports of agricultural products and labor-intensive manufactured products from the developing countries. It seems odd that the gains from trade among industrial countries in industrial products have not been extended to the developing countries when their products are competitive with either the industrial or agricultural products of the industrial countries.

The present round of General Agreement on Tariffs and Trade (GATT) negotiations provides an opportunity for reducing the barriers to trade in labor-intensive industrial products, such as textiles, and in farm products that cannot be competitively produced in temperate zones, such as sugar and numerous fruits and vegetables. The additional foreign exchange earnings made possible by lower trade barriers would permit the developing countries to obtain modern farm inputs at the lowest possible cost. There would be less need to engage in high-cost production of such inputs if the developing countries had ready access to them in international markets.

Reducing Waste. It is often stated that a large part of the world's food supply is lost through waste. According to *Time*, "At least one-quarter of the world's food disappears between the field and the table."[28] *Newsweek* perhaps went even further: "it is estimated that Americans waste up to 25 percent of the food they buy. And if the amount of food that contributes to obesity is taken into account, the figure goes as high as 50 percent."[29]

The *Newsweek* estimate of waste and excess eating is rather surprising, to put it mildly. Based on purchases at the retail level, the estimated daily per capita consumption in the United States as of 1969–71 was 3,330 calories. The estimated daily requirement has been set at about 2,650 calories.[30] Thus, if 50 percent of consumption consists of waste and excess eating, *Newsweek* has apparently revised daily calorie requirements down to 1,665, although no support was given for such a revision.

Undoubtedly there is substantial waste in food harvesting, distribution, and marketing, just as there is in automobile production or magazine publication. But after some effort to discover how waste has been measured, I conclude that we simply do not know how much waste actually occurs, either in the world as a whole or in the developing countries. In one sense, I wish that food waste in the developing countries did average 25 percent; a concerted effort to reduce such waste to 15 percent could probably be mounted at less cost than a program to increase food production by 10 percent.

Waste occurs—in the United States and elsewhere. But to eliminate it completely would almost certainly be uneconomic. And I find it hard to believe that the poor rural people of the world are not sensitive to the problems of waste and do not take the necessary steps to avoid it. People who collect cow dung or human excrement for use as fertilizer are not likely, in my opinion, to permit overall losses of food supply to average 25 percent or more between harvest and consumption, if such losses could be easily eliminated.

We need far more information than now exists on the extent of waste and the variety of measures that could reduce waste. But until we have much more information, it is inappropriate to heap blame upon the world's poor people for not solving problems that may not exist or could only be solved by a radical change in technology and a very large increase in investment.

---

28 *Time*, November 11, 1974, p. 78.

29 *Newsweek*, November 11, 1974, p. 67.

30 World Food Conference, United Nations, *Assessment of the World Food Situation, Present and Future*, E/CONF. 65/3, 1974, p. 51.

A Brief Summary

The necessary conditions for significant increases in food production in the developing countries are well known. The main conditions include a major expansion of agricultural research in the developing countries themselves, an adequate supply of modern inputs required to increase yields, the improvement and expansion of the irrigated area, incentives to farmers to make the required changes (including the expansion of the cultivated area), and improvements in transportation, marketing, and processing institutions and facilities. In addition, increased investment in human capital and improved communications is desirable, not only because of its contribution to increased agricultural output but also because of the need to assist farm people in the long-run adjustments they must make to economic growth.

Space limitations have prevented me from more than noting the importance of the expansion and improvement of marketing, transportation, and processing and of increased investment in human capital. The role of human capital in the developing countries has been ably presented by Theodore W. Schultz in his *Transforming Traditional Agriculture*.[31]

---

[31] Theodore W. Schultz, *Transforming Traditional Agriculture* (New Haven, Conn.: Yale University Press, 1964), especially Chap. 12.

8
POSSIBILITY AND PERFORMANCE

The possibility of significantly improving the food consumption of the poorer people of the world clearly exists. The world does not lack the resources required, nor are there biological or technical factors that would prevent us from realizing this desirable objective.

A strong case can be made that the major barriers to significant improvements in the per capita food supply of the developing countries are political in nature. The barriers are not primarily economic, except as economic matters affect both domestic and international political decisions. Neither are they scientific; the productivity of agricultural research institutions has been well documented. Nor do the barriers arise from the intractability, ignorance, or laziness of hundreds of millions of farmers around the world. If any of us found ourselves on a three-acre farm in India and had to feed ourselves and our families from the output of that farm, the probability of our starving would be substantial. Most of the poor farmers of the world make very efficient use of their limited resources.[1] They have shown both the willingness and the capacity to adopt new seed varieties and complex production technologies and to do so very promptly when profitability is evident.

But the governments of both the developing and the industrial countries must modify their approaches to long-run food problems if performance in the future is to be an improvement over the past. In saying this, I do not intend to denigrate what has been achieved over the past two decades in developing countries. The fact that food production has more than kept pace, although only slightly, with a population growth rate of about 2.5 percent annually in the developing

---

[1] Theodore W. Schultz, *Transforming Traditional Agriculture* (New Haven, Conn.: Yale University Press, 1964), Chap. 3.

market economies since 1952 is a significant achievement. The population growth rates of the developing countries have exceeded any experienced in the United States in this century, even during the baby boom after World War II.

Reducing the Birth Rate

The governments of the developing countries must be encouraged to realize that there can be no significant improvements in per capita food supply without declines in birth rates and reductions in population growth rates. Unless their birth rates are reduced, most of the efforts they are making to maintain a rate of growth in food production of 3 percent annually will simply provide approximately the current level of food consumption for a lot more people. If population growth remains at 2.5 percent annually, a 3 percent growth in food production would increase per capita food supplies by only 12 percent in a quarter of a century, that is, by the year 2000. And there is no certainty that a 3 percent rate of growth in food production could be maintained indefinitely.

As important and desirable as it is to achieve a reduction in birth rates in the developing countries, I believe that the United States and other industrial countries can play only a very limited role. The United States should continue its present policy, namely, to undertake research, both basic and applied, to improve contraceptive techniques, and to provide technical assistance when requested for establishing family planning programs. We should emphasize research on contraceptive techniques that are both simple and cheap, that require a minimum of input by the medical profession, and that can be made available in the most remote village in the world. It is important that we use all available means that can be used quietly and in a noncoercive manner to induce developing countries to face up to their population problems. But we should always remember that the subject is a delicate one requiring enormous tact and patience.

An encouraging development at the World Food Conference in 1974 was the unanimous acceptance of a resolution entitled "Achievement of a desirable balance between population and food supply." The resolution had the support of twenty-two developing countries, including India, Pakistan, Bangladesh, Egypt, Burma, and Mexico. The resolution called "on all governments and on people everywhere . . . to support, for a longer-term solution, rational population policies ensuring to couples the right to determine the number and spacing of births, freely and responsibly, in accordance with national needs within the context of an overall development strategy." [2] While one might have preferred the resolution without the last clause, the resolution directly related the growth of demand for food to population growth and recognized that "it is becoming increasingly difficult to meet the food needs of a rapidly growing world population."

Obviously, much more than elimination of governmental restraints on family planning or positive encouragement by governments of family planning is required to achieve a significant reduction in birth rates. Governments must also meet certain basic social needs such as rudimentary health services, reduced infant mortality, increased literacy, and a dependable food supply. In other words, they must help create the economic and social environment in which smaller families will be desired. Unless families have reasons for desiring fewer children, there is little likelihood that they will have fewer children.

There are a number of hopeful signs that the transition to lower birth rates is now underway in many developing countries. The Population Council has estimated that there were fifteen developing countries in which the birth rate declined by five to fifteen per thousand population during the 1960s. Except for Egypt, Sri Lanka (formerly Ceylon), South Korea, Taiwan, and West Malaysia, the fifteen countries had populations of less than 10 million. It was estimated that in eight additional countries there were possible declines in birth rates of five to nine per thousand, and this group included several with populations of twenty million or more—China, Turkey, Brazil, and Colombia.[3]

The Political Will

I am cautiously optimistic that the food supply situation of the developing countries will continue to improve over the coming decades. If I had as much confidence in the political process in both the industrial and developing countries as I do in the farmers of the world, I would drop the qualification "cautiously."

It is not at all clear that the industrial countries, either directly or through international aid agencies, will move promptly enough and with sufficient resources to expand the world's agricultural research. Foreign economic assistance does not appear to be high on the list of

---

[2] *Resolutions Adopted by the Committees of the World Food Conference* (Rome: Food and Agriculture Organization, November 1974), CL 64/INF/12, p. 18.

[3] Bernard Berelson, *World Population: Status Report 1974*, Reports on Population/ Family Planning of the Population Council, no. 15, January 1974, p. 9.

priorities of any of the industrial countries. What we are witnessing in our own Congress—its unwillingness to provide resources and to provide them on terms suitable for the solution of these pressing problems—is duplicated in many other countries. Only Canada, through the International Development Research Centre, appears to have set up the proper institutional arrangements. Unless there is an important change in our own approaches to assisting agriculture in the developing countries, we may well look back in 1985 and discover that Canada has contributed far more than we have.

Similarly, it is not at all obvious that the developing countries have either the political will or the administrative capacity to undertake the measures required to expand food production. Only the developing countries themselves can do anything to reduce the rate of population growth. So far one can have only limited optimism about their performance over the next decade.

All too many developing countries attempt to use governmental institutions and authority to carry out functions that would be much better left to the market. Rigid import controls, price ceilings, and governmental ownership or control of farm input industries do not contribute to increased farm production and often have negative influences. Most developing countries do not have the required administrative capacities to operate a rigidly controlled economy— and certainly not while maintaining a modicum of freedom.

But before we become too pessimistic about the performance of governments in the developing countries, we should remember that at least some of these countries responded very positively to the food stringencies of the mid-1960s. It is quite probable that the next few years will see similar responses by many governments. The problem may well be not how governments will react over the next few years but whether, once food supplies are more ample again (as I am confident they will be), they will relax their efforts, as they did in 1970 and 1971. Such a response together with, some years later, unfavorable climatic conditions in some major area of the world will result in another crisis or near crisis.

A paragraph from the World Food Conference's *Assessment of the World Food Situation* merits quoting in full:

> In recent years the prevailing view of the world food situation and prospects has swung from pessimism in 1965–66 to optimism in the "green revolution" years from 1967 to 1970 or so, and subsequently back again to pessimism. It is essential that the present widespread concern, which has arisen from . . . recent events . . ., should be directed to

the longer-term problems and lack of concern following a few years of good harvests.[4]

Need for Continuing Attention

World food problems are continuing ones, at least until the per capita incomes of the developing countries increase substantially above their present levels. Somehow it must be recognized that efforts to solve them must be long run in nature. It should be understood that measures or programs started now will need to continue until at least the end of this century.

Norman Borlaug, who received the Nobel Peace Prize in 1970 for his contributions to the development of high-yielding varieties of grain, remarked several years ago that these new varieties would not solve the food problems of the developing countries but that they could buy time for those problems to be solved if the time were used effectively.

> The green revolution has won a temporary success in man's war against hunger and deprivation; it has given man a breathing space. If fully implemented, the revolution can provide sufficient food for sustenance during the next three decades. But the frightening power of human reproduction must also be curbed; otherwise the success of the green revolution will be ephemeral only.[5]

It cannot be said that the world has used the time since 1967 at all effectively. The same mistakes should not be made again. The stakes are too high.

---

[4] World Food Conference, United Nations, *Assessment of the World Food Situation, Present and Future*, E/CONF. 65/3, 1974, p. 29.

[5] Norman Borlaug, "The Green Revolution, Peace and Humanity," speech given when he received the Nobel Peace Prize, December 10, 1970; reprinted by the Population Reference Bureau, Washington, D.C., Selection no. 35, January 1971, p. 8.

Cover and book design: Pat Taylor

RECENT STUDIES IN FOREIGN AFFAIRS

World Food Problems and Prospects by D. Gale Johnson first investigates the causes of the large increase in food prices in 1973–74 and of the shortfalls in food supplies in several low-income countries. Then, turning to the future, the author takes up such questions as: Can world food production at least keep pace with population growth? What roles should agricultural research, grain reserves, and food aid play in U.S. food policy?

Johnson finds no limitations in resources or technology to prevent the world's population from being better fed in the future than it was in the years immediately prior to 1972. He also finds that the required expansion in food supplies can come where it is needed, in the low-income countries. Large-scale food aid from the grain-exporting regions, though useful in emergencies, is not an effective long-run answer for these countries, he notes, and might indeed worsen their situation.

Although optimistic about the potential, Johnson questions whether governments will make the long-term commitments necessary to realize that potential. The requirements for expanding food production are well understood—more research, ready supplies of modern farm inputs such as fertilizer, more irrigation, and adequate incentives for farmers. However, according to the author, past experience indicates that when current food shortages are eased by a year or two of good harvests, governments may once again give low priority to policies for promoting more rapid growth in per capita food supplies in the low-income countries.

D. Gale Johnson is professor of economics, vice president of the university, and dean of the faculties at the University of Chicago. Formerly president of the American Farm Economic Association (1964–65), he has also served with the President's National Advisory Commission on Food and Fiber (1965–67) and the Commission on Population Growth and the American Future (1970–72).

$3.00

 American Enterprise Institute for Public Policy Research
1150 Seventeenth Street, N.W., Washington, D. C. 20036